Cyrus Thomas

The Cherokees in Pre-Columbian Times

Cyrus Thomas

The Cherokees in Pre-Columbian Times

ISBN/EAN: 9783337191399

Printed in Europe, USA, Canada, Australia, Japan

Cover: Foto ©ninafisch / pixelio.de

More available books at **www.hansebooks.com**

Fact and Theory Papers.

NUMBER IV.

THE CHEROKEES IN PRE-COLUMBIAN TIMES

BY PROF. CYRUS THOMAS

Fact and Theory Papers.

THE CHEROKEES
IN
PRE-COLUMBIAN TIMES

BY

PROF. CYRUS THOMAS

NEW YORK:
N. D. C. HODGES, PUBLISHER.
47 LAFAYETTE PLACE
1890

PREFACE.

The present little work, which is based chiefly upon data obtained while in charge of the mound explorations carried on by the United States Bureau of Ethnology, is presented to the public as indicative of the direction in which the more recent investigations in this line appear to lead.

I am under obligations to Major J. W. Powell for his kind permission to refer to the data obtained by the Bureau, bearing upon the questions discussed; but I must be held alone responsible for the views presented. The speculative theories advanced are, of course, but tentative, yet are believed by the author to accord more nearly with the facts ascertained than any suggestion, relating to the subject, which he has seen.

C. T.

Washington, July, 1890.

THE CHEROKEES
IN
PRE-COLUMBIAN TIMES.

CHAPTER I.

The present paper is an attempt by the writer to trace back the history of a single Indian tribe into the prehistoric or mound-building age. For this purpose the Cherokees have been selected, partly because of their isolated position geographically and linguistically, and partly because the data bearing upon the questions that arise in such an investigation are probably more complete than those relating to any other tribe of the mound section.

Although the scope is thus limited, there are certain facts relating to the mound region and the aboriginal inhabitants thereof, considered generally, which must be taken into account in studying the history of any tribe of this region.

The history of the Western Continent is supposed to begin with the discovery by Columbus, all that antedates that event being considered archæologic or prehistoric. While this is correct in the general sense in which it is used, yet the history of the different sections and different tribes begins with the first knowledge of them obtained by Europeans. The border-line, therefore, between the historic and prehistoric eras, varies in date when referred to the different sections and peoples. For example: history tells us nothing of what was transpiring in the area now called Ohio for a hundred hears after Cortez landed in Mexico. If it be possible to ascertain this, it must be sought in the traditions of the aborigines, the ancient monuments, and other prehistoric data of that area.

It is well known that when the various sections of this country were first visited by Europeans, they were found occupied by Indian tribes; while, on the other hand, there is no historical or other evidence, unless it be found in the monuments, that any other race or people than the Indians ever occupied this region. (The possibility of an Irish, Welsh, or Northmen pre-Columbian settlement is not at the present time taken into consideration, as it has no bearing on the subject now under discussion.) These tribes all belonged relatively to the same state of culture, which was of a grade inferior to that of the more advanced nations of Mexico and Central America.

Though not recorded in written or printed tomes, these aboriginal tribes must have had a history which still lived to some extent in their traditions, languages, customs, arts, beliefs, and relics, when the whites first became acquainted with them. These languages, customs, etc., though belonging to a plane much lower than that which ethnologists will allow us to call civilized, were not the growth of a season or a lifetime, but of centuries. If they exhibit tribal or ethnic peculiarities, it may be taken for granted that these peculiarities attained their growth subsequent to the separation of the stock into the tribes among which they are found. If they are local or confined to certain geographical areas, it is reasonable to assume that they were adopted by the tribes after reaching these localities. For example: the peculiarities of the civilization of Mexico and Central America, as seen at the time of the discovery of these countries, must be considered indigenous, so long as we are unable to trace them to other sections or other peoples,—a conclusion adopted by leading historians and antiquarians. The same thing is true to a more limited extent in regard to the subdivisions of these comprehensive groups, and affords some basis for estimating the period of occupation.

Those habits, customs, or arts common among savage peoples, of course teach nothing in regard to the occupants of any special locality, except to indicate their culture status. It is therefore to those which are local or ethnic that we must look for guidance in our search.

A second fact relating to the mound region generally is, that the ancient remains found in it, though presenting various types and numerous important differences, probably the result of different local or tribal customs, are evidently the work of peoples in about the same stage of culture. But to this and other general lessons taught by the monuments there will be occasion to call attention further on.

In order to clearly understand the position of the Cherokees relative to the other tribes in the mound area, we refer briefly to the linguistic distribution of these tribes when they first became known to the whites.

Stretching along the Atlantic coast from the mouth of the St. Lawrence to Pamlico Sound, and extending westward to the Mississippi, was the great Algonkin family, with its numerous divisions and branches. In the midst of this great linguistic sea, occupying most of what is now New York, and extending westward on both sides of the Lakes to Michigan (with a closely allied and also a distant offshoot— the latter the Cherokees—in the region of Carolina), was the Huron-Iroquois family, with its various branches. About the head waters of the Mississippi, and reaching westward far out upon the plains and southward to the Arkansas River, was the Dakotan family. Spread over the Gulf States was the Muskokee group. Add to these the vestiges of other stocks found driven, so to speak, into the corners here and there, and we have a condition that could not have been of mushroom growth, but the outcome of centuries. It is quite probable that the family stems migrated from other sections; but the splitting into branches and dialects took place, in part at least, after reaching the area in which these stocks were found. One proof of this is seen in the grouping and geographical distribution of the comprehensive families over the continent.

Judging by the growth of languages in Europe, although the cases are not exactly parallel, centuries must be allowed for this local development. It is said by those best qualified to judge, that the shifting, changing, and tribal development known to have taken place among the Dakotas of the North-west alone, must have required three or four centuries in advance of the Columbian discovery. The necessary inference to be drawn from this is, that the tribes, or rather families of tribes, found inhabiting this "mound region" by the first European explorers, had occupied substantially the same area for hundreds of years previous thereto. Not that there was no shifting or changing of positions by tribes, for there can be no doubt that this occurred to a greater or less extent, but that the families or stocks mentioned, or most of them, were in the area included in the eastern half of the United States and Canada (which we designate in a broad sense the "mound region") for centuries preceding the advent of the white man. The same method of reasoning will apply, to some extent, to the growth of customs, as this must also have required time.

The result of this course of reasoning, which seems to be justified by the facts, is to force us to one of the following conclusions: 1st, That the mound-builders, if a different race or people from the Indians, disappeared from the mound area before the coming of the latter, and many centuries before the advent of the whites; or, 2d, That there was an overlapping of the two races, that is to say, they occupied the area jointly for some centuries; or, 3d, That the Indians were the authors of the ancient monuments. As it will be necessary in the course of this investigation to discuss the question of the authorship of some of these antiquities, the decision reached on this subject is important in this connection.

Turning now to the Cherokees, we will proceed with the special object of this paper.

It is conceded that there is no hope of reconstructing a systematic pre-Columbian history of any one of the tribes or peoples of the area under consideration. The utmost that can be expected is, by a careful and thorough correlation of the data, to throw some light into that past which has so long been considered as wrapped in impenetrable mystery. It is by no means probable that as much will be accomplished in regard to the past of the people of this region, as has been done for Mexico and Central America, yet it is the belief of the writer that much more is possible in this direction than has generally been supposed.

This tribe was for a long time a puzzling factor to students of ethnology, as they were in doubt whether to consider it an abnormal offshoot from one of the well-known Indian stocks or the remnant of some undetermined or otherwise extinct family. It now appears, however, to be the clearly settled opinion of linguists that the language is an offshoot of the Huron-Iroquois stock. This is an important fact in the study of the past, not only of this tribe, but also of the family with which it is connected, as it necessitates looking to the same point for the origin of both.

When the people of this tribe first became known to the Europeans, they were located in the mountainous region including the south-east corner of what is now Tennessee, the south-west portion of North Carolina, the north-west part of South Carolina, and a strip along the northern border of Georgia,—a section which they continued to occupy down to a recent date, and where a remnant may still be found.

THE CHEROKEES IN PRE-COLUMBIAN TIMES.

The first notice of them is found in the chronicles of De Soto's expedition, which speak of them as the "Chelaques" or "Achelaques," words which give more correctly the sound of the name they gave themselves than the modern Anglicized form "Cherokee." These early records locate them about the head waters of the Savannah River. The exact route of the Spanish expedition has not been satisfactorily determined; nevertheless it is conceded by those best qualified to decide, that, when De Soto encountered people of this tribe, he was somewhere about the head waters of the Savannah, probably in the north-eastern part of Georgia. It was in this section, presumably in western North Carolina, that John Lederer encountered them during his visit to this part of the continent in 1669-70, for there can be no longer any reasonable doubt that he alludes to them where he speaks of the Indians of the "Apalatian Mountains." Their subsequent history is too well known to require further mention here.

Their relation to the Iroquois indicates a northern rather than a southern or south-western origin. This seems to be confirmed by the few rays of light which tradition, the records, and archæology throw upon their past history. Haywood states, in his "Natural and Aboriginal History of Tennessee," that they "were firmly established on the Tennessee River or Hogohega (the Holston) before the year 1650, and had dominion over all the country on the east side of the Alleghany Mountains, which includes the head waters of the Yadkin, Catawba, Broad River, and the head waters of the Savannah,"—a statement borne out by the fact that as late as 1756, when the English built Fort Dobbs on the Yadkin, not far from Salisbury, they first obtained the privilege of doing so by treaty with Atacullaculla, the Cherokee chief. The same authority states that they formerly had temporary settlements on New River (the Upper Kanawha) and on the head waters of the Holston. In De

Lisle's maps, 1700 to 1712, Cherokee villages are located on the extreme head waters of the Holston and Clinch Rivers, as well as on and about the mouth of the Little Tennessee.

Their traditions in regard to their migrations are somewhat confused, and, like all Indian traditions, must be taken only with careful sifting, and where strengthened by corroborative evidence or well-marked indications of being ancient. Yet there is a uniformity in some respects which, independent of other evidence, would justify the assumption that they contain a vein of truth and have some basis of fact.

One of the most important of these is that mentioned by John Haywood in the work above named, in which they claim to have formerly lived in the Ohio valley, and to have constructed the Grave Creek mound and other earthworks in that section. This author's statement is as follows:—

"The Cherokees had an oration in which was contained the history of their migrations, which was lengthy." This related "that they came from the upper part of the Ohio, where they erected the mounds on Grave Creek, and that they removed hither [East Tennessee] from the country where Monticello is situated." This tradition of their migrations was, it seems, preserved and handed down by their official orators, who repeated it annually in public at the national festival of the green-corn dance. Haywood adds, "It is now nearly forgotten;" and Dr. D. G. Brinton informs us, in "The Lenape and their Legends," that he has endeavored in vain to recover some fragments of it from the present residents of the Cherokee nation.

Haywood asserts, probably from original statements made to him, that "before the year 1690 the Cherokees, who were once settled upon the Appomattox River in the neighborhood of Monticello, left their former abodes, and came to the West. The Powhatans are said by their descendants to have once been a part of this nation. The probability is that a migration took place about or soon after the year 1632, when the Virginians suddenly and unexpectedly fell upon the Indians, killing all they could find, cutting up and destroying their crops, and causing great numbers to perish by famine. They came to New River and made a temporary settlement, and also on the head of the Holston."

It is obvious that in this passage the author has given his conclusion based on the "oration" mentioned, connecting with it the historical event of the sudden onslaught by the Virginia settlers upon the Indians, in 1632. That his deduction in this respect is erroneous if intended to apply to the whole tribe, is apparent from the following facts: first, because it is evident that a portion, at least, of the tribe was located in their historic seat, in and about East Tennessee and western North Carolina, when De Soto passed through the northern part of Georgia in 1540, as it is admitted that the "Chelaques" or "Achelaques" mentioned by the chroniclers of his expedition were Cherokees; second, because John Lederer, who visited this region in 1669-70, speaking of the Indians of the "Apalatian Mountains,"—doubtless the Cherokees, as he was at that time somewhere in western North Carolina,—says, in his "Discoveries," "The Indians of these parts are none of those which the English removed from Virginia, but were driven by an enemy from the northwest and invited to fix here by an oracle, as they pretend, above four hundred years ago;" third, from what is shown by the archæologic evidence which will be introduced further on.

The language of Lederer indicates that he had heard substantially the same tradition as that of which Haywood speaks. An important addition, however, is the supposed date of this migration, which this author says was "above four hundred years" preceding the date at which he writes (1671-72), which would place it in the latter part of the thirteenth century. The tradition as given by Haywood brings them from the valley of the Upper Ohio; that by Lederer, from the north west,—a close agreement as to the direction of their former home.

It is doubtful whether any importance is to be attached to Haywood's statement, that there was formerly a settlement in the vicinity of Monticello, Va. It is possible, that, during the migration toward the south-east, a party or clan broke off from the main body of the tribe, and settled in that region, where they remained until the general attack by the whites in the early part of the seventeenth century. Mr. Royce, in his paper on the "Cherokee Nation of Indians," in the "Fifth Annual Report of the Bureau of Ethnology," gives a tradition preserved among the Mohicans (or Stockbridges) which he suggests may have some bearing on this question. It is that "many thousand moons ago, before the white men came over the great water, the Delawares dwelt along the banks of the river that bears their name. They had enjoyed a long era of peace and prosperity, when the Cherokees, Nanticokes, and some other nation whose name had been forgotten, envying their condition, came from the south with a great army, and made war upon them. They vanquished the Delawares, and drove them to an island in the river. The latter sent for assistance to the Mohicans, who promptly came to their relief, and the invaders were in turn defeated with great slaughter, and put to flight. They sued for peace, and it was granted on condition that they should return home and never again make war on the Delawares or their allies. These terms were agreed to, and the Cherokees and Nanticokes ever remained faithful to the conditions of the treaty."

Passing over the improbability that a marauding party forced to fly would stop and sue for peace, the tradition may, after all, have some basis of fact, as there is nothing improbable in the supposition that a band of Cherokees went north from the banks of the Holston or Kanawha as far as the Delaware on a war expedition.

What is supposed to be the earliest notice of this tribe through the settlers of Virginia is that given by the historian Burke. According to this author, Sir William Berkely, governor of that State, sent out, in 1667, an expedition consisting of fourteen whites and an equal number of friendly Indians, under command of Capt. Henry Blatt, to explore the mountainous region to the west. After seven days' travel from their point of departure at Appomattox, they reached the foot of the mountains. The first ridge they crossed is described as being neither very high nor steep; but the succeeding ones, according to their statement, "seemed to touch the clouds," and were so steep that an average day's march while passing over them did not exceed three miles. After passing beyond the mountains they came into a level region, through which a stream flowed in a westward course. Following this for a few days, they reached some old fields and recently deserted Indian cabins. Beyond this point their Indian guides refused to proceed, alleging that not far away dwelt a powerful tribe that never suffered strangers who discovered their towns to return alive: consequently the party was forced to return. It is believed by some authorities that the powerful nation alluded to in the narrative of this expedition was the Cherokees.

It is probable that the point reached was what is now Floyd or Montgomery County, and that the Indians so much dreaded were located on New River or the extreme head waters of the Holston.

Another tradition related by Haywood is that one party or band of the tribe came to their mountain home from the neighborhood of Charleston, S.C., and settled south of the Little Tennessee, near what is now the Georgia line. The people of this branch called themselves "Ketawanga," and came last into the country

Another tradition is, that when they first came into this region they found it uninhabited with the exception of a Creek settlement on the Hiawassee River. Ramsey, upon what authority is not known, says this was a Uchee settlement.

It is apparent that all these traditions, except that relating to a clan from the neighborhood of Charleston, point to some northern locality as the former home of the tribe, and that in this respect they correspond with the linguistic indications. But these do not exhaust the evidence bearing on this question, as there is a tradition of another nation, and in this case one of the best known and most reliable of all Indian traditions, which agrees with the others in this respect. This is the Delaware legend regarding their ancestral home and migrations. The earliest writer who gives a detailed statement of it is the Rev. Charles Beatty, who visited the Delaware settlements in Ohio in 1767. According to this authority, "of old time their people were divided by a river, nine parts of ten passing over the river and one part remaining behind; that they knew not, for certainty, how they came to this continent; but account thus for their first coming into these parts where they are now settled; that a king of their nation, where they formerly lived, far to the west, left his kingdom to his two sons; that the one son making war upon the other, the latter thereupon determined to depart and seek some new habitation; that accordingly he sat out accompanied by a number of his people and that, after wandering to and fro for the space of forty years, they at length came to Delaware River where they settled three hundred and seventy years ago. The way they keep an account of this is by putting a black bead of wampum every year on a belt they keep for that purpose."

The reason for mentioning this brief notice of the tradition, rather than relying entirely on the fuller account given below, is that it mentions a date purporting to be derived from the Indians.

The tradition as given by Heckewelder, who heard it from the Delawares themselves, and had the advantage of their interpretation and comments, is as follows:—

"The Lenni Lenape (according to the tradition handed down to them by their ancestors) resided many hundred years ago in a very distant country in the western part of the American continent. For some reason which I do not find accounted for, they determined on migrating to the eastward, and accordingly set out together in a body. After a very long journey and many nights' encampment by the way, they at length arrived on the *Namaesi-Sipu*, where they fell in with the Mengwe, who had likewise emigrated from a distant country and had struck upon this river somewhat higher up. Their object was the same with that of the Delawares: they were proceeding on to the eastward until they should find a country that pleased them. The spies which the Lenape had sent forward for the purpose of reconnoitring, had, long before their arrival, discovered that the country east of the Mississippi was inhabited by a very powerful nation, who had many large towns built on the great rivers flowing through their land. Those people (as I was told) called themselves *Talligeu* or *Tallegewi*. . . . Many wonderful things are told of this famous people. They are said to have been remarkably tall and stout; and there is a tradition that there were giants among them, people of a much larger size than the tallest of the Lenape. It is related that they had built to themselves regular fortifications or intrenchments, from whence they would sally out, but were generally repulsed. I have seen many of the fortifications said to have been built by them, two of which in particular were remarkable. One of them was near the mouth of the River Huron, which empties itself into the Lake St. Clair on the north side of that lake, at the distance of about twenty miles north-east of Detroit. This spot of ground was, in the year 1776, owned and occupied by a Mr. Tucker.

The other works, properly intrenchments, being walls or banks of earth regularly thrown up, with a deep ditch on the outside, were on the Huron River, east of the Sandusky, about six or eight miles from Lake Erie. Outside of the gateway of each of these two intrenchments, which lay within a mile of each other, were a number of large flat mounds, in which, the Indian pilot said, were buried hundreds of the slain Tallegwi whom I shall hereafter, with Col. Gibson, call Alligewi. Of these intrenchments, Mr. Abraham Steiner, who was with me at the time when I saw them, gave a very accurate description, which was published at Philadelphia in 1789 or 1790, in some periodical work the name of which I cannot at present remember.

"When the Lenape arrived on the banks of the Mississippi, they sent a message to the Alligewi to request permission to settle themselves in their neighborhood. This was refused them, but they obtained leave to pass through the country and seek a settlement farther to the eastward. They accordingly began to cross the Namaesi-Sipu, when the Alligewi, seeing that their numbers were so very great, and in fact they consisted of many thousands, made a furious attack upon those who had crossed, threatening them all with destruction if they dared to persist in coming over to their side of the river. Fired at the treachery of these people and the great loss of men they had sustained, and, besides, not being prepared for a conflict, the Lenape consulted on what was to be done,—whether to retreat in the best manner they could, or to try their strength and let the enemy see that they were not cowards, but men, and too highminded to suffer themselves to be driven off before they had made a trial of their strength and were convinced that the enemy was too powerful for them. The Mengwe, who had hitherto been satisfied with being spectators from a distance, offered to join them on condition that after conquering the country they should be entitled to share it with them.

Their proposal was accepted, and the resolution was taken by the two nations to conquer or die.

"Having thus united their forces, the Lenape and Mengwe declared war against the Alligewi, and great battles were fought, in which many warriors fell on both sides. The enemy fortified their large towns and erected fortifications, especially on large rivers or near lakes, where they were successfully attacked and sometimes stormed by the allies. An engagement took place in which hundreds fell, who were afterwards buried in holes, or laid together in heaps and covered over with earth. No quarter was given, so that the Alligewi at last, finding that their destruction was inevitable if they persisted in their obstinacy, abandoned the country to the conquerors, and fled down the Mississippi River, from whence they never returned.

"The war which was carried on with this nation lasted many years, during which the Lenape lost a great number of their warriors, while the Mengwe would always hang back in the rear, leaving them to face the enemy. In the end the conquerors divided the country between themselves. The Mengwe made choice of the lands in the vicinity of the Great Lakes and on their tributary streams, and the Lenape took possession of the country to the south. For a long period of time, some say many hundred years, the two nations resided peacefully in this country, and increased very fast. Some of their most enterprising huntsmen and warriors crossed the great swamps, and, falling on streams running to the eastward, followed them down to the great bay river (meaning the Susquehanna, which they call the great bay river from where the west branch falls into the main stream), thence into the bay itself, which we call Chesapeake. As they pursued their travels partly by land and partly by water, sometimes near and at other times on the great salt-water lake, as they call the sea, they discovered the great river which we call the Delaware."

If this tradition has any foundation in fact (and it certainly seems to have), there must have been a people to whom the name "Tallegwi" was applied, for on this a large portion of it hangs. Who were they? Is it possible to trace them to any tribe of modern times? The supposition of Col. Gibson mentioned by Heckewelder, that the name survives in "Alleghany," applied to the chief river and mountains of western Pennsylvania, is not generally accepted by linguists of the present day. Heckewelder was of opinion that "Talligewi" was a word foreign to the Algonkin, which was simply adopted by the Delawares. Dr. Brinton says, "It is not necessarily connected with Alleghany, which may be pure Algonquin. He (Heckewelder) says, 'Those people called themselves Talligeu or Talligewi.' The accent as he gives it, 'Talligéwi,' shows that the word is Tallike, with the substantive verb termination, so that Talligewi means 'He is a Tallike' or 'It is of (belongs to) the Tallike'" ("The Lenape and their Legends," p. 320).

Heckewelder's account, no doubt colored to some extent by his own interpretation, varies slightly from the tradition as given in the "Walam Olum." He interprets *Namaesi Sipu* by "Mississippi" because of his opinion that the migration was from the west. It is more probable that Mr. Hale is correct in assuming that it was some portion of the great river of the north (the St. Lawrence) which connects together and forms the outlet for the Great Lakes, possibly that portion which connects Lake Huron with Lake Erie. If this supposition be accepted, it would lead to the inference that the Talamatan—the people who joined the Delawares in their war with the Tallegwi—were Hurons or Huron-Iroquois previous to separation. Mr. Hale's views on this question are expressed in the *American Antiquarian*, April, 1883, as follows:—

"The country from which the Lenape migrated was Shinake, the 'land of fir-trees;' not in the west, but in the far north,—evidently the woody region north of Lake Superior. The people who joined them in the war against the Allighewi (or Tallegwi, as they are called in this record) were the Talamatan, a name meaning 'not of themselves,' whom Mr. Squier identifies with the Hurons, and no doubt correctly, if we understand by this name the Huron-Iroquois people as they existed before their separation. The river which they crossed was the Messeesipe, the 'Great River' beyond which the Tallegwi were found 'possessing the east.' That this river is not the Mississippi is evident from the fact that the works of the mound-builders extended far to the westward of the latter river, and would have been encountered by the invading nations if they had approached it from the west long before they had arrived at its banks.

"The great river was apparently the Upper St. Lawrence, and most probably that portion of it which flows from Lake Huron to Lake Erie, and which is commonly known as the Detroit River. Near this river—according to Heckewelder, at a point west of Lake St. Clair, and also at another place just south of Lake Erie—some desperate conflicts took place. Hundreds of slain Tallegwi, as he was told, were buried under mounds in that vicinity. This precisely accords with Cusick's statement that 'the people of the great Southern Empire had already penetrated to Lake Erie' at the time the war began. Of course, in coming to the Detroit River from the region north of Lake Superior, the Algonquins would be advancing from the west to the east. . . . The passage already quoted from Cusick's narrative informs us that the contest lasted perhaps one hundred years. In close agreement with this statement, the Delaware record makes it endure during the term of four head chiefs, who in succession presided in the Lenape councils."

The passages of the Delaware record which refer to the Tallegwi, as translated by Dr. Brinton, are as follows.

"They (the Lenape) separated at Fish River (Nemassipi, sometimes written Mistissippi); the lazy ones remained there.
Cabin-Man was chief; the Tallegwi possessed the east.
Strong-Friend was chief; he desired the eastern land.
Some passed on east; the Talega ruler killed some of them.
All say in unison, 'War, war!'
The Talamatin, friends from the north, come and all go together.
The Sharp-One was chief; he was the pipe-bearer beyond the river.
They rejoiced greatly that they should fight and slay the Talega towns.
The Stirrer was chief; the Talega towns were too strong.
The Fire-Builder was chief; they all gave to him many towns.
The Breaker-in-Pieces was chief; all the Talega go south.
He-has-Pleasure was chief; all the people rejoice.
They stay south of the lakes; the Talamatin friends north of the lakes."

Further on, and referring to a later period, are the following verses:—

"14. The Rich-Down-River-Man was chief, at Talega River.

18. Snow-Hunter was chief; he went to the north land.
19. Look-About was chief; he went to the Talega mountains.
20. East-Villager was chief; he was east of Talega.

40. At this time whites came on the Eastern sea.

42. Well-Praised was chief; he fought at the south.
43. He fought in the land of the Talega and Koweta.

45. White-Horn was chief; he went to the Talega,
46. To the Hilini, to the Shawnees, to the Kanawhas."

The reasons for identifying the Tallegwi or Talega of this tradition with the Cherokees, which will be more fully referred to hereafter, are briefly as follows: 1st. The very close agreement in sound between *Tsalake*, the name the Cherokees gave themselves, and *Tallegwi* or *Talega* as given in the tradition; 2d, The fact that the traditions of the Cherokees refer to the region of the Upper Ohio as their former home; 3d, The statement of Bishop Ettwein that the last of the Cherokees were driven from the Upper Ohio about the year 1700 (see Brinton's "Lenape and their Legends," p. 18); 4th, The testimony of the mounds; and, 5th, The apparent identification of the two peoples in the "Walam Olum" itself in verses 42 and 43, Part V., where it states that

> "Well-Praised was chief; he fought at the south.
> He fought in the land of the Talega and Koweta."

As this part of the record refers to a much later period than that heretofore quoted, a date subsequent to the appearance of the whites on the continent (verse 40, Part V.), there can be no doubt that it alludes to the Tallegwi in their southern home, to which, as stated in verse 59, Part IV., they had been driven. This supposition is apparently confirmed by the fact that it connects with them the Koweta, or Creeks. This, together with the statement that the fighting was at the south, would seem to imply they were then in their mountain home or historic seat. It is probable, as will be shown hereafter, that where it is stated, in verses 19 and 20,

> "Look-About was chief; he went to the Talega mountains;
> East-Villager was chief; he was east of Talega,"

their position in the Kanawha valley is referred to, where, as the evidence indicates, they halted for some time on their way south.

CHAPTER II.

HAVING thus followed back the chain by the light of history and tradition, we turn next to the evidence derived from the mounds.

Although it cannot be stated positively that no tribe except the Cherokees occupied this Appalachian region between 1540 and 1690, still the evidence and indications leading to that conclusion are so strong as to justify us in assuming it to be correct. It is possible that clans or small parties from other tribes may have taken up their abode temporarily with these mountain Indians; but, so far as history informs us and the remains indicate, a single instance of the kind only is known. It is therefore a fair presumption that such mounds or other works of this area, not constructed by the whites, which indicate contact with European civilization, if there be any, are to be attributed to the Cherokees.

One of the ancient burial-places in Caldwell County, N.C., explored by the agents of the United States Bureau of Ethnology, is described as being a burial-pit in the form of a triangle, the two long sides 48 feet each, and the southern base 32 feet, in which the bodies and accompanying articles were deposited and then covered over, but not so as to raise any distinct mound above the natural surface of the ground, or, if so, it had settled to the level of the latter. The depth of the original excavation, the sides of which could be distinctly traced, varied from two and a half to three feet. In this pit were twenty-seven skeletons arranged as follows: nine lying horizontally on their backs on the bottom of the pit, with nothing over them except the dirt (these were buried separately); four were in a sitting posture, and over each a small beehive-shaped vault of cobblestones; four buried two and two in vaults, but lying horizontally at full

FIG. 1.

length; and ten or more in one group, which, from their arrangement in regard to each other, the explorers believed must have been interred at one time, the skeleton of the principal personage of the group resting horizontally on his face on the bottom of the pit. Under the head of this skeleton was a large engraved shell gorget shown in the figure (Fig. 1). Around the neck were a number of large-sized shell beads, probably the remains of a necklace; at the sides of the head, near the ears, five elongate copper beads, or rather small cylinders, varying in length from one and a half to four inches, part of the leather thong on which the smaller ones were strung yet remaining in them. These beads were made of thin copper cut into strips, and then rolled up so as to bring the edges together on one side in a straight line. The plate out of which they were made was as smooth and even as though it had been rolled. Under the breast of the same skeleton was also a piece of copper. The arms were partially extended, the hands resting about a foot from the head. About each wrist were the remains of

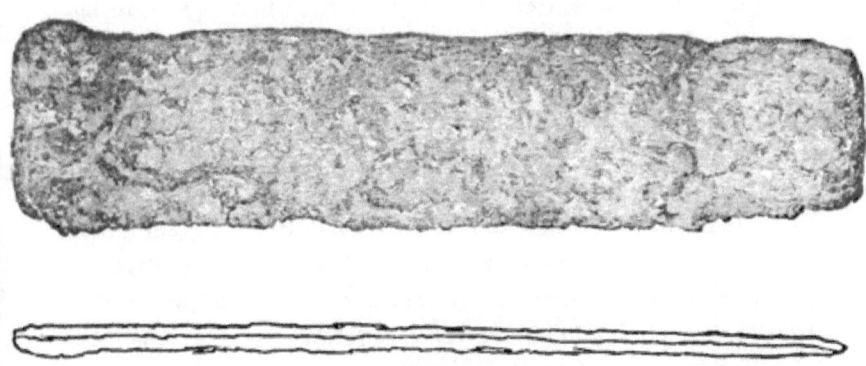

FIG. 2.

a bracelet composed of alternate beads of copper and shell. At his right hand were four iron specimens much corroded, but sufficiently distinct to indicate their form and use. One of these was in the form of a thin celt; another, about five inches long, is apparently part of the blade of a long slender cutting or thrusting implement of some kind, as a sword, dagger, or knife (shown in Fig. 2); another is part of a round awl-shaped implement, a small part of the bone handle in which it was fixed yet remaining attached to it. A careful analysis of the iron of these implements has been made by Professor Clark of the United States Geological

Survey, who decides that it is not meteoric. Under the left hand of the same skeleton was another engraved shell, the concave side upward, and filled with shell beads of various sizes.

Around and over the skeleton of this chief personage, with their heads near his, were nine other skeletons. Under the heads of two of these were two engraved shells. Scattered over and between the skeletons of this group were numerous polished celts, discoidal stones, copper arrow-points, plates of mica, lumps of paint, etc.

That these iron articles cannot be attributed to an intrusive burial is evident from the preceding description. They were found at the bottom of the pit, which had been dug before depositing the bodies. With them were engraved shells, polished celts, and other relics of this character, and all were deposited with the principal personage who had been buried in the mound. There were, in fact, no indications whatever of intrusive burials here.

As it is conceded that neither the Indians nor the more civilized tribes of Mexico and Central America were acquainted with the art of manufacturing iron, the presence of these iron articles in the mound indicates contact with the civilization of the Old World. Moreover, a careful examination of the copper cylinders will probably satisfy any one that the plate of which they were made had been rolled or regularly hammered by other than stone implements, and that the strips had been cut into proper shape with some hard metallic instrument. It is reasonable, therefore, to conclude that this burial-pit was dug, and the bodies deposited, subsequent to the discovery of America by Columbus, and in all probability after the date of De Soto's expedition. As the Cherokees alone inhabited this particular section from the time of De Soto's expedition until it was settled by the whites, it is more than probable that the burials were made by them.

This is an important step in the attempt to trace backward the history of this tribe, as it is seemingly the link which crosses the border-line between the historic and prehistoric eras. It should therefore be well sustained by other data before being used as a basis for further advance; but this is not wanting.

On the same farm as the preceding was another burial-place, also explored by the agents of the Bureau of Ethnology, of which an account is given in the "Fifth Annual Report." In this case we have a true mound, although of comparatively little height. This was almost a true circle in outline, thirty-eight feet in diameter, but not more than a foot and a half in height above the natural surface of the ground. Thorough excavation, however, revealed the fact that the builders of the mound had first dug a circular pit of the same diameter, with perpendicular margin, to the depth of three feet, on the bottom of which they deposited their dead, some in little stone vaults and some without any stone enclosure, and covered them over with earth, raising the mound above the pit.

A plan of the pit, showing the stone vaults and skeletons after the removal of the dirt, is given in Fig. 3. The beehive-shaped vaults were built of water-worn bowlders, with merely sufficient clay to hold them in place.

No. 1 indicates a stone vault standing exactly in the centre of the pit. In this case a small circular hole a little over three feet in diameter, and extending down three feet below the bottom of the pit, had been dug, the body or skeleton placed perpendicularly upon its feet, and a wall built up around it, converging, after a height of four feet was reached, so as to be covered at the top by a single soapstone slab of moderate size. On the top of the head of the skeleton, and immediately under the capstone, were several plates of silver mica, which had evidently been cut with some rude implement. Although the bones were much decayed, yet they were retained in an upright position by the dirt which filled the vault,—an indication that the flesh had been removed before burial, and earth packed around the skeleton as the vault was built up.

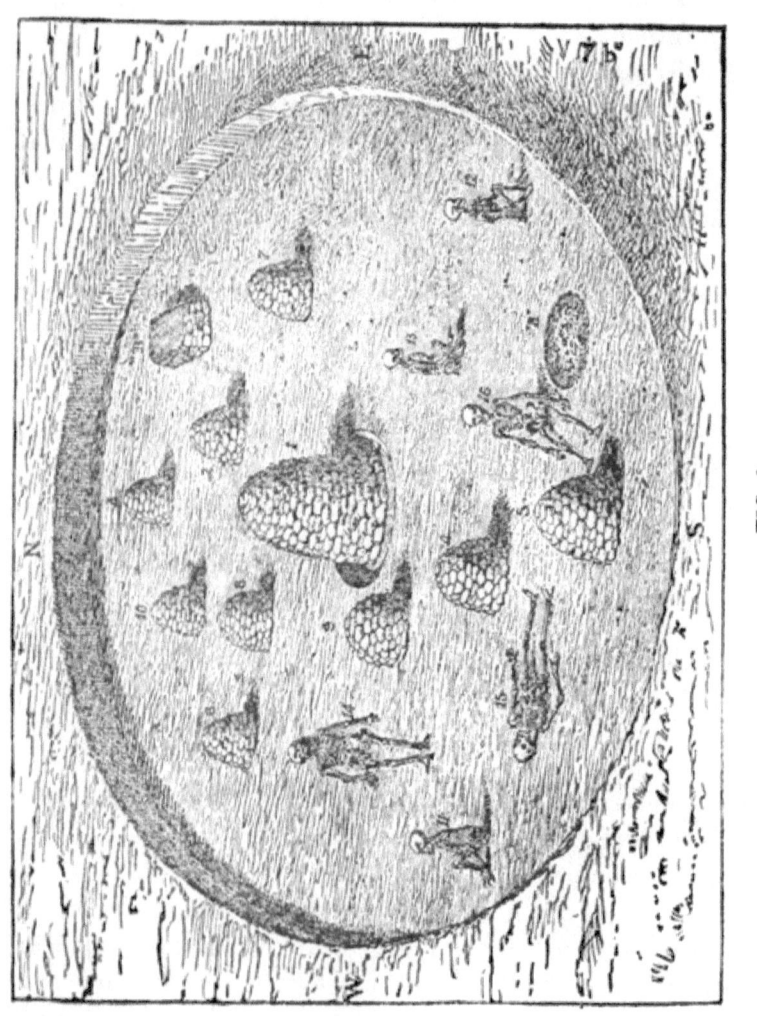

FIG. 3.

Nos. 2, 3, 4, 5, 6, 7, 8, 9, and 10 are small vaults, each covering a skeleton placed in a sitting or squatting posture on the bottom of the pit. Nos. 11, 12, and 13 are uncovered skeletons in a squatting posture. Nos. 14 and 15 are uncovered skeletons lying horizontally on the bottom of the pit. No. 16 is an unenclosed squatting skeleton of unusually large size: *A*, a quantity of black paint in lumps; and *B*, a cubical mass of water-worn bowlders built up solidly and regularly, twenty-four inches long, eighteen inches wide, and eighteen inches high, but with no bones, specimens of art, coals, ashes, or indications of fire on or about it. Many of the stones of the little vaults and the earth immediately around them, on the contrary, bore unmistakable evidences of fire; in fact, the heat in some cases had been so intense as to leave its mark on the bones of the enclosed skeletons,—another indication that the flesh had been removed before burial.

The only relic found deserving notice here was a soapstone pipe near the mouth of No. 16.

The proximity of this mound to the Triangle, the occurrence of the pit, and the similarity in the modes of burial, are sufficient to justify us in attributing them to one and the same people. Two hundred yards east of the Triangle was another low mound, covering a circular pit similar to that described. In this were twenty-five skeletons and one stone heap. Some of the skeletons were in a sitting posture, covered with stone vaults, others unenclosed. Some were stretched horizontally on the bottom of the pit, unenclosed. Four of the latter were lying together, with large stones resting on their legs below the knees.

In a different part of the same county, another similar circular burial-pit was explored, in which, besides the separate sitting and horizontal skeletons, there was a kind of communal grave similar to that in the Triangle. As there can be no reasonable doubt that all these are the burial-places of one tribe, and there are no indications of intrusive burials, it is legitimate to consider them together, and to draw inferences in regard to the customs of the authors from what is found in any one.

Referring to the account given in the "Fifth Annual Report of the Bureau of Ethnology," it is seen that the following articles were found buried with the skeletons of the last-mentioned pit alone: one stone axe; forty-three polished celts; nine vessels of clay, including four pots and two food-cups, the handle of one representing an owl's head, and that of the other an eagle's head; thirty-two arrow-heads; twenty soapstone pipes, mostly uninjured; twelve discoidal stones; ten rubbing-stones; one broken soapstone vessel; six engraved shells, some of the designs on them like that shown in Fig. 1; four shell gorgets; one sea-shell (*Busycon perversum*) entire, and two or three broken ones; five very large copper beads; a lot of shell fragments, some of them engraved; a few rude shell pins made from the *columellæ* of sea-univalves; shell beads and a few small copper beads.

It is evident, from the mode of burial and the articles found, that these works cannot be attributed to white men of post-Columbian times. Can they be attributed to the Indians found inhabiting this region at the time of the advent of the whites? If the evidence justifies this conclusion, we may then attribute them without hesitancy to the Cherokees.

Lawson, who travelled through North Carolina in 1700, states that "the Indians oftentimes make of a certain large sea-shell a sort of gorge, which they wear about their neck in a string, so it hangs on their collar, whereon is sometimes engraven a cross or some odd sort of figure which comes next in their fancy." Beverly, in his "History of Virginia," evidently alluding to the same custom, says, "Of this shell [the conch] they also make round tablets of about four inches in diameter, which they polish as smooth as the other, and sometimes they etch or grave thereon circles, stars, a half-moon, or any other figure suitable to their fancy." Adair states, in his "History of the American Indians," that the priest wears a breastplate made of a white conch-shell, with two holes bored in the middle of it, through which he puts the ends of an otter-skin strap, and fastens a buck-horn white button to the outside of each.

Here, then, is evidence of a custom among the Indians precisely similar to that which prevailed among the moundbuilders of the region to which reference has been made. Nor does the comparison stop with the general resemblance

FIG. 4.

in customs; for among the shells found in the burialmounds mentioned was one with a cross engraved upon it, and on others were engraved figures that might be readily taken for stars and half-moons (Fig. 4). Moreover, while some are "engraved," others are "smooth," without any devices upon them; and all are pierced with holes for inserting strings by which to hang them about the neck. They are usually made from *Busycon perversum*, which is designated in common parlance a "conch."

That shells of this kind, bearing precisely similar engraved designs, were in use among the veritable mound-builders, is proven by the fact that they have been found in mounds of some of the most important groups of Georgia, Tennessee, and elsewhere. This fact is sufficient of itself to show that the North Carolina burial-places alluded to belong to the mound-building age. If these shell ornaments are the work of Indians, as appears from the statements of the above-named writers, they must have been used by the Cherokees, and buried with their dead.

The author last above quoted says, that at the fall of the leaf the Indians gather hickory-nuts, "which they pound with a round stone, upon a stone, thick and hollowed for the purpose." Quite a number of precisely such stones as here mentioned, "thick and hollowed" at the ends, were found in the mounds of Caldwell County, N.C. All who examined them ascribed them, without hesitancy, to the use mentioned by Adair.

Another fact not mentioned in the preceding description of these mounds and burial-places is, that in one,—the circular pit,—mixed with those having heads of the ordinary form, were some eight or ten skeletons with heads of elongate form, due to artificial pressure.

This furnishes strong evidence that the people who buried here were Indians. It is true, it was not a custom of the Cherokees to compress the head, but it was of their neighbors and hereditary foes, the Catawbas As this is the only instance of skulls of that form being found in the mounds of this section, it is possible they were captives from that tribe; but why buried here, unless they had been adopted by the Cherokees, is a question difficult to answer.

In the mounds and burial-places mentioned were also found a large number of nicely carved soapstone pipes, usually with the stem made in connection with the bowl, though some of them are without this addition, consisting only of the bowl, with a hole for the insertion of a cane or wooden stem.

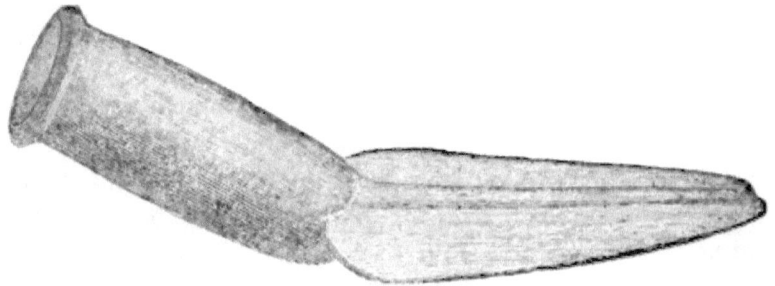

FIG. 5.

By turning to Adair's "History of the American Indians," we find this statement: "They [the Indians] make beautiful stone pipes, and the Cherokees the best of any of the Indians, for their mountainous country contains many differ-

FIG. 6.

ent sorts and colors of soils proper for such uses. They easily form them with their tomahawks, and afterwards finish them in any desired form with their knives; the pipes used with the fire, when they become quite hard. They are often a full span long, and the bowls are about half as long again as those of our English pipes. The fore-part of each commonly runs out with a sharp peak two or three fingers broad and a quarter of an inch thick."

Not only were pipes made of soapstone found with the stem carved in connection with them, as indicated in the above quotation, but two or three were obtained of precisely the form mentioned by Adair, with the fore-part running out in front of the bowl; and others of the same form have been found in West Virginia, Ohio, and elsewhere. Some of the forms, including one from a mound in Sullivan County, East Tenn., are shown in Figs. 5 and 6. As will be seen, one of these, of which numerous examples were found, has a very modern appearance,—a form which was first adopted in England in the time of Queen Elizabeth. It may be remarked, in passing, that the mound in Sullivan County, Tenn. (shown in Fig. 37, "Fifth Annual Report of the Bureau of Ethnology"), belongs to the same type as that of Caldwell County, N.C. Here, however, instead of a pit, a circular wall some three or four feet high is built on the natural surface of the ground, and the bodies or skeletons are seated in regular order on this natural surface, after charcoal and ashes have been strewn over it, and over each a little vault built.

Haywood, in his "Natural and Aboriginal History of Tennessee," says, "Mr. Brown, a Scotchman, came into the Cherokee nation in the year 1761, and settled on the Hiawassee River or near it. He saw on the Hiawassee and Tennessee the remains of old forts, about which were axes, guns, hoes, and other metallic utensils. The Indians at that time told him that the French had formerly been there and built these forts."

During the year 1883 one of the assistants of the Bureau of Ethnology explored this particular section which Haywood refers to. An overflow and a change in the channel of the river brought to light the remains of old habitations and numerous relics of the people who formerly dwelt there. Moreover, this was in the precise locality where tradition and the statement of the Cherokees located a Cherokee town. Digging was resorted to in order to complete the exposure which the water had begun. The only object in view in referring to this exploration is to note some of the articles found: ten discoidal stones precisely like those from the mounds of Caldwell County, N.C.; nine strings of glass beads; a number of shell beads exactly like those from the mounds; a number of flint arrow-points; one soapstone pipe; some pieces of smooth sheet copper; three conical copper ear pendants precisely of the pattern of some found in one of the Carolina mounds; three buttons of modern type; one small brass gouge; fragments of iron articles belonging to a bridle; one bronze sleigh-bell; one stone awl or drill; fragments of a soapstone pot; one soapstone gorget; several polished stone celts similar to those found in the Carolina mounds; grooved stone axes; a piece of sheet lead.

This admixture of articles of civilized and savage life confirms the statement made by Haywood, at least so far as regards the early presence of white people in this section. It follows, from what has been presented, that the Indians living here after the appearance of the whites must have been Cherokees; and the fact that the implements and ornaments of aboriginal manufacture found here are throughout precisely like those obtained from the mounds mentioned, affords a very strong proof that the latter are to be attributed to the same people.

Additional and perhaps stronger evidence, if stronger be needed, that the people of this tribe were the authors of most of the ancient works in western North Carolina and East Tennessee, is to be found in certain discoveries made by the Bureau assistants in Monroe County, Tenn.

A careful exploration of the valley of the Little Tennessee River from the point where it leaves the mountain to its confluence with the Holston was made, and the various mound groups located and carefully surveyed.

Here, on the exact sites of the "Over-hill towns," as shown by Henry Timberlake's map of 1765, using the map of the same region by the Geological Survey as a mears of comparison, were found mound groups; not in a general sense only, but in the order given and at the points indicated, a group for each town, and in the only habitable spots the valley, for this distance, affords. Commencing with the large island immediately below the mouth of Tellico River at the west end of Timberlake's map, we see the town of Mialoqua, partly on the island, and partly on the south bank. Referring to the Bureau map, which will appear in the general report of mound explorations, we see that the mounds are also partly on the island, and partly on the south bank. On the latter map, group No. 2 corresponds with "Toskegee" of Timberlake's map; No. 3, with "Tommotley;" No. 4, with "Toqua;" No. 5, with "Tennessee;" No. 6, with "Chote;" No. 7, with "Settacoo;" No. 8, with "Half-way Town;" No. 9, with "Chilhowey;" and No. 10, with "Tellassee." Such remarkable coincidence cannot be attributed to mere chance. There is also the additional fact that the evidences of village sites which must have been left by the Cherokee towns were found only about the groups, though careful search was made by the Bureau agents along the valley.

As these mounds, when explored, yielded precisely the kind of ornaments and implements used by the Cherokees, it is reasonable to believe they built them.

Ramsey also gives a map of the Cherokee towns in his "Annals of Tennessee;" but his list, although corresponding, so far as it goes, with the order given by Timberlake, evidently refers to a date corresponding with the close of their occupancy of this section. Bartram gives a more complete list. This includes some towns on the Holston (his "Cherokee") River and some on the Tellico Plains, the localities corresponding with mound groups discovered by the Bureau agents. For example: some three or four groups are in the region of the Tellico Plains, and five or six on the Little Tennessee below Fort Loudon, and on the Holston near the junction of the two. One large mound and a group were discovered on the "Big Island" mentioned by Bartram, on which he locates a town, but fails to give the name.

The largest of these groups is situated on the Little Tennessee above Fort Loudon, and corresponds with the position of the ancient "Beloved town of Chota" ("Great Chote" of Bartram) as located by tradition and Timberlake's map. According to Ramsey, at the time the pioneers, following in the wake of Daniel Boone near the close of the eighteenth century, were pouring over the mountains into the valley of the Watauga, a Mrs. Bean, who was captured by the Cherokees near Watauga, was brought to their town at this place, bound, and taken to the "top of a mound" to be burned, when Nancy Ward, then exercising in the nation the functions of the "beloved" or "pretty woman," interfered, and pronounced her pardon. Ramsey does not give his authority for this statement. but, in all probability, obtained the information from the descendants of Mrs. Bean, who, as the writer knows, were residing in Hawkins County as late as 1850, and probably at the present time. "Nancy Ward" probably received her English name from some white family that resided for a time in that section.

During the explorations of the mounds of this region by the Bureau agents, a peculiar type of clay beds was found in several of the larger tumuli. These were always saucer-shaped, varying in diameter from six to fifteen feet and in thickness from four to twelve inches. In nearly every instance there was a series one above another, with a layer of coals and ashes between. A series usually consisted of from three to five beds, sometimes only two, decreasing in diameter from the lowest one upwards. These apparently marked the stages of the growth of the mound, the upper one always being near the surface.

The large mound on the supposed site of Chota, and possibly the one on which Mrs. Bean was about to be burned, was thoroughly explored, and found to contain a series of these clay beds, which always show the action of fire. In the centre of some of these were found the charred remains of a stake, and about them the usual layer of coals and ashes; but in this instance immediately around where the stake stood were the charred fragments of human bones. There may be no connection between this fact and Ramsey's statement, yet the coincidence is suggestive.

The burials in this mound, which was a large one, some twelve feet high, were at various depths, from two and a half to nine feet, and, although the series of clay beds indicated growth, there was nothing to indicate separate and distinct periods, or to lead to the belief that any of these were intrusive. On the contrary, the evidence is pretty clear that all these burials were by one tribe or people. It is believed that no satisfactory evidence of intrusive burials has been discovered in this entire Appalachian region. By the side of nearly every skeleton in this mound were one or more articles, as shell masks, engraved shells similar to those heretofore mentioned, shell pins, shell beads, perforated shells, discoidal stones, polished celts, arrow-heads, spear-heads, stone gorgets, bone implements, clay vessels, and copper hawk-bells. The last-named articles were with the skeleton of a child found at the depth of three feet and a half. They are precisely of the form of the ordinary sleigh-bell of the present day, but with pebbles and shell beads for rattles.

That this child belonged to the people by whom the other burials, some of which were at less depth, were made, there is no reason to doubt; and that the bells indicate contact with Europeans must be conceded.

In another mound a little farther up the river, one of a group marking the site of one of the "Over-hill towns," were discovered two carved stone pipes of a comparatively modern Cherokee type.

During the fall of 1888, a farmer of East Tennessee, while examining a cave with a view of storing potatoes in it during the winter, unearthed a well-preserved human skeleton, which was wrapped in a large piece of cane matting. This, which measures about six by four feet, is quite pliant, and, with the exception of a rent in the corner, perfectly sound. It has a broad, submarginal stripe of red running around it. Enclosed with the skeleton was a piece of cloth made of flax, about fourteen by twenty inches, almost uninjured, pliant, but apparently unfinished. The stitch in which it is woven is precisely the same as that imprinted on pottery shown in Fig. 96 in Mr. Holmes's paper on "Mound-Builders' Textile Fabrics" ("Third Annual Report of the Bureau of Ethnology"). Although the earth in the cave contains salts which would aid in preserving any thing buried in it, these articles cannot be assigned to any very ancient date, especially as there were with them the remains of a dog from which the skin had not all rotted away. These were in all probability placed here by the Cherokees of modern times, and form a link between the historic and prehistoric times not easily broken.

Another important find was made in this locality by one of the Bureau agents in 1889. This is a small stone on which some characters have been rudely etched, and is shown in Fig. 7, on the next page. An examination by those familiar with the subject will probably soon satisfy them that some of the characters, if not all, are letters of the Cherokee alphabet. As the presence of the stone in the mound cannot be attributed to an intrusive burial, it is evident that the mound must have been built since 1820, that Mr. Guess was not the author of the Cherokee alphabet, or that the stone is a fraud. The mound in which this was found is described as follows:—

"The Tipton group is situated on the north side of the Little Tennessee, about two miles from Morganton. No. 3 of this group, which stands about one hundred feet from No. 2, is of small size, measuring twenty-eight feet in diameter and about five feet in height. Some large trees," says Mr. Emmert, the Bureau agent, "were standing on the mound, and Mr. Tipton informed me that he had cut other trees off of it forty years ago, and that it had been a cluster of trees

FIG. 7.

and grape-vines as far back as the oldest settler could recollect. There was an old stump yet in the centre, the roots of which ran down in the mound almost or quite to where the skeletons were found. . . . Having worked to the bottom, I found here nine skeletons lying at full length on the natural surface, with faces up, and surrounded by dark-colored earth. No. 1 (as shown in the diagram which accompanies his report) was lying with head to the south; while No. 2, close by the side of it, had the head to the north, and feet almost touching the head of the other. On the same level, but apart from the preceding, were seven other skeletons lying closely side by side, heads all to the north, and all in a line. No relics of any kind were found with any of the skeletons except No. 1. Immediately under the skull and jaw-bones were two copper bracelets, an engraved stone (Fig. 7), a small drilled stone, a single copper bead, a bone instrument, and some small pieces of polished wood. The earth about the skeletons was wet, and the pieces of wood were soft and colored green by contact with the copper bracelets. These bracelets had been rolled up in something which crumbled off when they were taken out, but whether buckskin or bark I was unable to decide. The engraved stone was lying partially under the skull. I punched it with my steel prod on the rough side in probing, before I reached the skeletons."

As soon as the collections made by Mr. Emmert during this exploration were received at the office in Washington, a member of the Bureau was sent to the field where Mr. Emmert was at work, to learn the whole history of the find. This course was taken by the Bureau merely as a means of being fortified with all possible evidence as to the facts of the find being as stated. The examination by the person sent confirmed the statement by Mr. Emmert in every particular. This, therefore, necessitates one of two conclusions,—that the mound was thrown up since 1820, or that some one was at work on the Cherokee alphabet before Mr. Guess's time. But this is a question which has no bearing on the present discussion.

CHAPTER III.

WHAT has been presented is probably sufficient to convince any unbiassed mind that the Cherokees were mound-builders, nevertheless there is other evidence of a more general character which serves to show that the builders of the East Tennessee and North Carolina mounds were contemporaneous with the authors of the works of other sections.

Proof that in general the mound-builders were Indians would, as a matter of course, have a strong bearing on the case under discussion, but this would require too much space to be introduced here. The following extracts from Major J. W. Powell's article on "Prehistoric Man in America," in the *Forum* of January, 1890, will give what is now becoming the settled conclusion of most of the leading archæologists of the present day:—

"The research of the past ten or fifteen years has put this subject in a proper light. First, the annals of the Columbian epoch have been carefully studied, and it is found that some of the mounds have been constructed in historical time, while early explorers and settlers found many actually used by tribes of North American Indians: so we know many of them were builders of mounds. Again, hundreds and thousands of these mounds have been carefully examined, and the works of art found therein have been collected and assembled in museums. At the same time, the works of art of the Indian tribes, as they were produced before modification by European culture, have been assembled in the same museums, and the classes of collections have been carefully compared. All this has been done with the greatest painstaking, and the mound-builders' arts and the Indians' arts are found to be substantially identical. No fragment of evidence remains to support the figment of theory that there was an ancient race of mound-builders superior in culture to the North American Indians. . . . It is enough to say that the mound-builders were the Indian tribes discovered by white men."

Once it is admitted that the mound-builders were Indians, it requires much less proof to carry conviction that a particular tribe was accustomed to erect such structures. There are, however, two facts which seem to carry back the Cherokees to the mound-building age, even independently of this general argument.

The first of these to which attention is called is that afforded by a certain class of stone graves or cists found in great numbers in some sections. These cists, usually designated "box-shaped stone graves," are formed of rough unhewn slabs or flat pieces of stone, thus: first, in a pit some two or three feet deep and of the desired dimensions, dug for the purpose, a layer is placed to form the floor; next, similar pieces are set on edge for the sides and ends, over which other slabs are laid flat, forming the covering; the whole, when finished, making a rude box-shaped coffin or sepulchre. Sometimes one or more of the six faces are wanting; occasionally the bottom consists of a layer of water-worn bowlders; sometimes the top is not a single layer, but other pieces are laid over the joints; and sometimes they are placed in the fashion of shingles. They vary in length from fourteen inches to eight feet, and in width from nine inches to three feet.

Now, it happens that quite a number of graves of this particular type are found on the site of one of the "Over-hill towns" heretofore mentioned, and others are scattered over parts of the Cherokee district. As the location of those about the village site is such as to justify the belief that they were contemporaneous with the existence of the village, we must conclude that the authors of the graves of this type, and the Cherokees, were contemporaneous. Additional proof of this is found in the seemingly conclusive evidence, which is too lengthy to be introduced here, that the graves of this form found south of the Ohio are due to the Shawnees. The well-known fact that the Cherokees and Shawnees were long hereditary and bitter foes, almost constantly at war with each other, would seem to forbid the above supposition that a Shawnee colony was living in connection with a Cherokee village; yet the following historical items furnish a satisfactory explanation.

Haywood, in his "Natural and Aboriginal History of Tennessee," gives the following statement by Gen. Robertson: "In 1772 the Little Corn-Planter, an intelligent Cherokee chief who was then supposed to be ninety years of age, stated, in giving a history of his own nation, that the Savannechers, which was the name universally given by the Indians to those whom the English call Shawnees, removed from Savannah River, between Georgia and South Carolina, by permission of the Cherokees, to Cumberland, they having been attacked and almost ruined by a combination of several of the neighboring tribes of Indians; that many years afterwards a difference took place between the two nations, and the Cherokees, unexpectedly to the Shawnees. marched in a large body to the frontier of the latter."

There is, however, another item of evidence directly in point found in the following statement in Schoolcraft's

"History of the Indian Tribes:" "A discontented portion of the Shawnee tribe from Virginia broke off from the nation which removed to the Scioto country in Ohio about the year 1730, and formed a town known by the name of 'Lulbegrud' in what is now Clark County (Kentucky), about thirty miles east of this place (Lexington). This tribe left this country about 1750, and went to East Tennessee, to the Cherokee nation." It is very probable that the stone graves about the site of the "Over-hill town" are due to this band.

The importance and bearing of this evidence in the present connection lie in the fact that numbers of graves of this type are found in mounds, some of which are of comparatively large size, and connected with works which no one hesitates to attribute to the true mound-building age. Sometimes they are arranged in these tumuli in two, three, and even four tiers. Not only are they found in mounds of considerable size, but they are also connected with one of the most noted groups in the United States; namely, the one on Col. Tumlin's place, near Cartersville, Ga., known as the "Etowah mounds," of which a full description will be found in the "Fifth Annual Report of the Bureau of Ethnology" and in Jones's "History of the Southern Indians." In the smallest of the three large mounds of this group were found stone graves precisely of the type described; not in a situation where they could be attributed to intrusive burial, but in the bottom layer of a mound some thirteen or fourteen feet high, with an undisturbed layer, two feet thick, of hard-packed clay above them. In them were found the remarkable figured copper plates and engraved shells which are described by the writer in the "Fifth Annual Report of the Bureau of Ethnology," also in *Science*. In singular corroboration of the idea here advanced, the only other similar copper plates were found in a stone grave at Lebanon, Tenn.; in a stone-grave mound at Mill Creek, southern Illinois; in a stone grave in Jackson County, Ill.; in a mound of Madison

County, Ill.; and in a small mound at Peoria, Ill.; not all, of course, attributed to Shawnees, but in stone graves or mounds, thus connecting them with the mound-building age, which is the only point with which we are at present interested.

Another important link in this discussion is found in the engraved shells, of which specimens were found in the mounds of North Carolina and East Tennessee attributable to the Cherokees.

The following list, showing localities where and circumstances under which specimens have been found, will suffice to show their relation to the mounds and stone graves: Lick Creek, and near Knoxville, E. Tenn., in mounds; near Nashville, Tenn., in mound, also in stone grave; Old Town, Franklin, and Sevierville, Tenn., in mounds; Bartow County, Ga., in stone grave in mound; Monroe County, E.Tenn., Lee County, Va., and Caldwell County, N.C., in mounds; near Mussel-Shoals, Ala., in cave; New Madrid, Mo., and Union County, Ill., in mounds; St. Clair County, Ill., in stone grave.

As a large number of these bear exactly the same carved designs as those found in the Cherokee mounds, the evidence seems conclusive that we must assign them to the same age. This, of course, connects the Cherokees with the mound-builders' era, and furnishes a justifiable basis for another backward step. But before attempting to take this, I add some information on the point now under discussion, gathered by Mr. James Mooney during his ethnological investigations among the Cherokees in behalf of the Bureau of Ethnology. This is given in a paper read before the Anthropological Society of Washington City.

"In connection with my work, at the instance of the Bureau of Ethnology, in the summer of 1887, I visited the East Cherokee reservation in western North Carolina. Being delayed over night at a small town called Webster, about twenty miles from the reservation, an opportunity was afforded to make the acquaintance of Capt. J. W. Terrell, the postmaster, an intelligent American, who in his younger days had been a trader among the Cherokees, and who has some knowledge of the language. In the course of our conversation he stated that about thirty years ago he had been told by an old Indian named Tsiskwaya that the Cherokees had built the mounds in their country, and that on the occasion of the annual green-corn dance it was the custom in ancient times for each household to procure fresh fire from a new fire kindled in the town-house. I afterward found that this Tsiskwaya had been regarded as an authority on such matters.

"Subsequently, in investigating the ceremonies of the green-corn dance, this statement was confirmed by another old man, who volunteered the additional information that it was customary to begin a mound on the occasion of this dance, when representatives of the seven gentes brought baskets filled with earth, which was placed in a common pile with appropriate ceremonies, and afterward added to by the labors of the common people. This man is somewhat unreliable, and his testimony would have little weight by itself, but it is of value in so far as it is borne out by the statements of others. It is proper to state, however, that he was one of the masters of ceremonies at the green-corn dance of 1887, so that he may reasonably be supposed to know something on that subject. Of curious interest in this connection is the fact that Miss Alice C. Fletcher witnessed a similar ceremonial mound-building at one of the secret rites of the Winnebagoes.

"But the most detailed statement as to the mounds was obtained afterward from Ayunini ('Swimmer'), who, although not an old man, is one of the most prominent Cherokee shamans and a general conservator of Indian knowledge, being probably better acquainted with the myths, traditions, and ceremonial formulas than any other man of the tribe. For some time he refused to talk, but this difficulty was finally overcome by appealing to his professional pride; and his stock of Indian lore proved so extensive, that I brought him to the house, and kept him with me most of the time. This aroused the jealousy of rivals, who took occasion to circulate damaging reports as to his honesty; but in every instance I found his statements borne out by other testimony or by general analogy. Making due allowance for the mythologic features, which rather serve to establish its traditional character, his account is probably as full and accurate as could be expected at this late day, and briefly is as follows:—

" 'The practice of building mounds originated with the Anintsi, and was kept up by the Ani-Kituhwagi. They were built as sites for town-houses (see Bartram's account of Cowe mound and town-house); and some were low, while others were as high as small trees. In building the mound, a fire was first kindled on the level surface. Around the fire was placed a circle of stones, outside of which were deposited the bodies of seven prominent men, one from each gens, these bodies being exhumed for the purpose from previous interments.'

"Swimmer said that his statement was obtained from a man who died in 1865, aged about seventy. Some time later, while talking with an intelligent woman in regard to local points of interest, she mentioned the large mound near Franklin, in Macon County, and remarked, 'There's fire at the bottom of that mound.' Without giving her any idea of what Swimmer had said, I inquired of her how the fire got there, when she told substantially the same story as she had obtained it from an old woman now dead. She was of the opinion that this fire existed only in the larger mounds; but I found on investigation that the belief was general that the fires still existed, and occasionally sent up columns of smoke above the tops of the mounds."

CHAPTER IV.

SUMMING up the evidence introduced, it leads to the following conclusions:—

1. That some of the Cherokees reached their historic seat before the year 1540, probably as early as the latter part of the thirteenth century.

2. That they came from some point to the north or northwest, apparently in the region of the Ohio River.

3. That some, if not all, of the mounds of western North Carolina and East Tennessee were built by the people of this tribe.

Assuming these points to be sufficiently established, let us see what evidence can be adduced indicating their line of migration.

If their former home was in the region of the Upper Ohio, and they stopped for a while on New River and the head waters of the Holston, their line of retreat was in all likelihood up the valley of the Great Kanawha. This supposition agrees also with the fact that no traces of them are found in the ancient works of Kentucky or middle Tennessee. In truth, the works along the Ohio River from Portsmouth (except those at this point) to Cincinnati, and throughout northern Kentucky, are different from the typical works of Ohio, and most of them of a type found in no other district. On the other hand, it happens, precisely in accordance with the theory advanced, that we find in the Kanawha valley, near the city of Charleston, a very extensive group of ancient works, stretching along the banks of the stream for more than two miles, consisting of quite large as well as small mounds, circular and rectangular enclosures, etc. A careful survey of this group has been made, and a number of the tumuli, including the larger ones, explored by the representatives of the Bureau of Ethnology.

The result of these explorations has been to bring to light some very important data bearing upon the present question. In fact, the discoveries made here seem to furnish the connecting link between some of the works of Ohio and those of East Tennessee and North Carolina ascribed to the Cherokees.

Subsequent to the preparation of the paper on the "Burial-Mounds of the Northern Section," published in the "Fifth Annual Report of the Bureau of Ethnology," further explorations and a careful resurvey of the group near Charleston were made. In order to show the bearing of the data obtained on the questions involved in this discussion, it is necessary to give somewhat detailed descriptions of some of the mounds explored.

Mound 15 of this group (for convenience the numbers in the original sketch are used) was sixty-five feet in diameter and five in height, though a considerable portion had been ploughed off in cultivating the soil. In the top was a basin-shaped fire-bed somewhat oval in outline, being about seven feet long and four feet wide. This was composed of a mixture of clay and ashes burned to a brick red on the upper side; but the under side had a black, greasy appearance. Below this was a similar bed, on and about which were numerous small fragments of bones, but too much broken and charred to show whether they were human or animal.

These basin-shaped beds remind us of those of similar form found in the mounds of East Tennessee, and present one indication of relationship between the mound-builders of the two sections.

Mound No. 18, about the same size as the preceding, contained a similar series of basin-shaped fire-beds, lying one below the other in the central portion. Below them, near the bottom of the mound, was a considerable bed of charcoal and ashes; and immediately under this, on the original surface of the ground, the fragments of a skeleton, with which were a number of broken arrow and spear heads.

Mound No. 1 of the group is of large size, measuring five hundred and twenty feet in circumference and thirty-three in height. This was explored by sinking a shaft twelve feet square to the bottom. At the depth of from three to four feet, in a bed of mixed clay and ashes, were three skeletons lying extended on their backs, doubtless intrusive burials. From this point downwards for twenty feet, nearly all of the material in the shaft consisted of the same mixed substances, so hard as to require the constant use of the pick. At the depth of twenty-four feet there was a sudden change to a much softer and darker-colored earth, in which were the casts and decayed fragments of poles and logs from six to twelve inches in diameter. These, together with fragments of bark, ashes, and animal bones which had been split lengthwise, continued through a layer of about six feet. At the depth of thirty-one feet a human skeleton was discovered lying prostrate, head north, the skull crushed but partly preserved by contact with a sheet of copper (only fragments of which remained) that probably once formed part of a head-dress of some kind. By enlarging and curbing, the shaft was extended to a diameter of sixteen feet. It was then found that a layer of elm-bark had been carefully spread, with the inner side up, upon the smoothed and well-packed surface of the ground. This had been covered with a layer a few inches thick of fine white ashes. On this the body was laid, and covered with similar bark.

Ten other skeletons, all buried in the same manner, were found at this point, arranged, five on each side, in a semi-circle around the central one just mentioned, with feet turned toward it. With each skeleton on the east side of the centre was a fine, apparently unused lance-head; and by the side of the northern one of these five, a fish-dart, three arrow-points, and some decayed mussel-shells. Nothing was found with the other five. With the central one, in addition to what has been mentioned, were six shell beads and a large lance-head.

But what interests us more at present is the fact that near the head of the latter was a conical vault of very hard clay, about four feet high and five feet in diameter. This was partially filled with rotten bark, human bones, and dark, decomposed matter. Immediately under this, but covered with clay, were two circular holes about sixteen inches in diameter, and four feet deep. A similar pair of holes was found at the head of each of the ten surrounding skeletons, ranging in depth from two to three feet, and in diameter from eight to twelve inches.

The little beehive vault, resembling so exactly in form and size those of North Carolina, although built of clay, is another indication of relationship between the mound-builders of the two sections. On the other hand, the burial between the layers of bark is precisely what is often found to be the case in the Ohio mounds, as appears from the following statements by Messrs. Squier and Davis in "Ancient Monuments:" "The course of preparation for the burial seemed to have been as follows: the surface of the ground was first carefully levelled, and packed over an area perhaps ten or fifteen feet square. This area was then covered with sheets of bark, on which, in the centre, the body of the dead was deposited, with a few articles of stone at its side, and a few small ornaments near the head. It was then covered over with another layer of bark, and the mound heaped above."

The individual or skeleton buried in the conical vault had probably been wrapped in bark.

That there was a wooden structure of some kind covering the area occupied by the skeletons is more than probable, as thus only can we account for the timbers. The holes mentioned may indicate the position of a former structure, but this had been removed before the burials took place. It would seem that most, if not all, of the burials took place at one time, and after the flesh had been removed.

Mound 21, known locally as the "Great Smith Mound," is the largest of the group, being a regular cone, thirty-five feet high, and one hundred and seventy-five feet in diameter at the base. This was explored by sinking a shaft to the bottom twelve feet in diameter. It is a double mound, or mound of two stages. The first building carried it to the height of twenty feet: after a considerable time had elapsed, another stage of work carried it to its present height. Near the top were some skeletons, probably intrusive burials. At the depth of twelve feet the explorers began to find the fragments and casts of logs, the first being that of a black-walnut log, which must have been nearly twelve inches in diameter and several feet in length. Further excavation made it apparent that these timbers were the remains of a wooden vault about thirteen feet long and twelve feet wide. From all the indications,—the casts of the posts and logs, the bark and clay lining, the fallen timbers, the bark of the roof, etc.,—it was inferred that the vault was constructed as follows: after the mound, which was at this time twenty feet high, had been standing for an indefinite length of time, a square pit, twelve by thirteen feet, was dug in the top to the depth of six feet; posts were then placed along the sides and ends, the former reaching only to the surface, but the central ones at the ends rising four feet higher; on the latter was placed the ridge-pole (the walnut log first encountered); the sides were plastered with a mixture of clay and ashes, and possibly lined with bark; the roof, which had fallen in, was made of poles, and covered with bark; over all was heaped the superincumbent mound fifteen feet in height.

In this vault were five skeletons, one lying prostrate on the floor at the centre. The other four had been placed, one in each corner, apparently in an upright position. All had been wrapped in bark. The central skeleton was very large, measuring a little over seven feet in length. Each wrist was encircled by six heavy copper bracelets. A fragment of the wrapping, preserved by contact with the copper, shows that it was black-walnut bark. A piece of dressed skin, which had probably formed the inner wrapping, was also preserved by the copper. Upon the breast was a copper gorget; by each hand were three flint lance-heads; near the right hand, a small hematite celt and a stone axe. Around the head, neck, and hips were about one hundred small, perforated sea-shells and some shell beads. Upon the left shoulder, lying one upon another, were three sheets of mica from eight to ten inches long, six to seven in width, and half an inch thick.

Further discoveries of badly decayed skeletons were made in carrying the shaft downward below the vault, but nothing with which we are at present concerned except the fact that among the articles obtained was the steatite pipe shown in Fig. 8.

The significance of this mound lies in the close resemblance it bears, in some respects, to the Grave Creek mound, which, according to the tradition of the Cherokees, was built by their ancestors. But at present no argument is based upon this part of the tradition. This latter giant tumulus is in the form of a regular cone, seventy feet high, and nearly three hundred in diameter at the base. A shaft sunk from the apex to the base disclosed two wooden vaults,—the first about half way down, and the other at the bottom. In the first or upper one was a single skeleton decorated with a profusion of shell beads, copper bracelets, and plates of mica. The lower vault, which was partly in an excavation made in the natural ground, was rectangular, twelve by eight feet, and seven feet high. Placed close together along each side and across the ends of the excavation were upright timbers or posts, which supported others thrown across to form the roof. In this vault were two human skeletons, one of which had no ornaments, while the other was surrounded

FIG. 8.

with hundreds of shell beads. In attempting to enlarge this vault, the workmen discovered around it ten other skeletons.

The similarity in the method of constructing the vaults is marked and peculiar. Wooden vaults are not uncommon; but those partially sunk in a pit, with the sides and ends formed of upright posts, are very rare, and are probably due to some peculiar custom, and indicate tribal identity of the builders. We notice also the presence, with one of the skeletons in each mound, of copper bracelets and plates of mica. In both a vault is built about midway the height.

Mound 31 of the Kanawha group presents some striking resemblances to the so-called "sacrificial mounds" of Ohio. It is somewhat flattened on top, three hundred and eighteen feet in circumference at the base, and twenty-five feet high. After passing through the top layer of soil, some two feet thick, a layer of clay and ashes one foot thick was encountered. Here, near the centre of the shaft, were two skeletons lying horizontally. These were probably intrusive burials. At the depth of thirteen feet, and a little north of the centre of the mound, were two large skeletons in a sitting posture, with their extended legs interlocked to the knees. Their arms were extended and their hands slightly elevated, as if they were together holding up a sandstone mortar which was between their faces. At the depth of twenty-five feet, and resting on the natural surface of the ground, was one of the so-called "altars," precisely similar to those found in some of the Ohio mounds. This, which was thoroughly traced, was found to be twelve feet long and a little over eight feet wide. It consisted of clay, apparently slightly mixed with ashes, the middle portion basin-shaped, and the margins sloping downwards and outwards; in other words, it was a typical "altar," similar to that shown in Fig. 32, "Ancient Monuments." The depth of the basin in the centre was a little over a foot, and the thickness of the bottom at this point about six inches. On this rested a compact layer of very fine white ashes from one to two feet thick, entirely covering this clay bed. Scattered through them were many water-worn bowlders from three to five inches in diameter, all bearing indications of exposure to intense heat; also fragments of charred bones, some of which were nearly destroyed by heat. The upper side of this clay bed or "altar" was burned to a brick red.

That this tumulus must be classed with the (so-called) "sacrificial mounds" of Ohio, will, it is presumed, be admitted without any objection. As the custom of building these clay structures, to which Messrs. Squier and Davis applied the name "altars," seems to have been peculiar to one class of Ohio mound-builders, we have here one very strong indication that the people who built the mounds of this Kanawha group belonged to the same tribe.

Mound 23 is of considerable size, measuring three hundred and twelve feet in circumference and twenty-five in height. It had never been disturbed in any way, and was the most pointed and symmetrical of the group.

As the discoveries made in it are important in this connection, the report of the Bureau explorer is given somewhat fully.

It was examined by sinking a large central shaft to the bottom. From the top to the depth of fifteen feet, the material passed through was an exceedingly hard, gray mixture, apparently of ashes and clay. At this depth casts of poles and timbers of various sizes were discovered, but all less than a foot in diameter, extending into the western and southern sides of the shaft. These casts and rotten wood and bark continued to increase in amount nearly to the natural soil, which was reached at the depth of twenty-five feet. The *débris* being removed, and the bottom of the shaft enlarged to fourteen feet in diameter, it was ascertained that these timbers had formed a square or polygonal vault, twelve feet across, and some eight or ten feet high in the centre. This had been built up in the form of a pen, the ends of the poles extending beyond the corners. The roof must have been sloping, as the ends of the poles used in making it extended downward beyond the walls on which they rested. On the floor of this vault, which corresponded with the original surface of the ground, were two adult skeletons, the bones of which, though but little decayed, were crushed and pressed out of position. No implement or ornament was found with them.

As the earth of this floor did not appear to be the natural soil, the shaft was carried down four feet farther. This revealed a pit, the lateral extent of which could not be determined, but which had been dug to the depth of four feet in the original soil. On the floor of this pit, at one side, arranged in a semicircle, were six small clay vaults in the shape of beehives, about three feet in diameter at the bottom, and the same in height.

They were made of clay and ashes mixed, very hard, and impervious to water. Possibly they had been allowed to dry before being covered with earth. They were partially filled with a dark, dry dust, apparently of some decayed substance. A few fragments of bones were found in them.

In the centre of the space around which these little vaults were arranged, but only two feet below the floor of the large wooden vault, were two small clay-lined cavities about the size and form of the ordinary water-jars from the Arkansas mounds. Possibly they were decayed, unburnt vessels which had been deposited here at the time of burial.

The bottom of the pit, which consisted of the natural deposit of yellow sand, was covered with a layer of charcoal and ashes two or three inches thick. This sand appeared to have been heated, from which it is inferred that the burning took place in the pit previous to the formation of the vaults.

The work was suspended at this stage, on account of extreme cold weather, but was recommenced the following season by running trenches from the sides into the shaft, and afterward carrying a tunnel in at the base. In one of these trenches, nine feet from the top, occurred a layer of soft earth, in which were numerous fragments of decayed timbers and bark, also casts of logs extending horizontally into the sides of the trench. These, it is presumed from what was afterward discovered, pertained to a wooden burial-vault. The tunnel carried in at the base was from the south side, ten feet wide, and eight feet high. For a distance of twenty feet it passed through the hard gray material of which the body of the mound was composed. Here the explorers suddenly encountered a deposit of soft earth in lenticular masses and of various colors, showing that it had been brought from the hillsides and bottoms near by. A short distance from this point they began to find the casts and remains of the timbers of the large central vault, but, before reaching the interior, passed over a small refuse-heap, evidently belonging to an age preceding the date of the building of the mound. As they entered the remains of the vault, they began to find tolerably well preserved human bones, but no whole skeletons. Seeing here indications of the pit before mentioned, the tunnel was carried downward four feet, disclosing five little clay vaults similar to those found on the other side, and, like them, placed in a semi-circle. It was now decided to remove and thoroughly explore about one-half of the mound. Many stone implements, some entire but most of them broken, seemingly by the action of fire, were scattered through the hard upper layer, also numerous single valves of mussels which had been used as digging-tools until they were worn from the outside entirely through.

There was a marked dissimilarity between the northern and southern sides of this mound, the former being a compact mass of variously colored soils from different points in the vicinity, in alternate horizontal layers. The separate loads of the individuals who carried this earth were plainly defined; and the different sizes of these small masses indicate that many persons, some much stronger than others, were simultaneously engaged in the work.

With the exception of the imperfect or broken specimens mentioned above, no remains of any kind were found in that portion of the mound above the fire-bed and north of the central shaft, and only two skeletons beneath it; while many interesting finds of implements were made all through the loose, ashy dirt of the southern part, and many skeletons below it. The amount of rotten wood and bark observed, and the positions of the casts of logs and poles, some of which extended downward four feet below the natural surface of the ground, render it probable that there was a wooden structure here twelve feet square and three stories high, or, what is more likely, three structures, one above another.

A foot above the natural surface, or twenty-four feet from the top of the mound, was a smooth horizontal layer of sand and ashes, interrupted by two heavy fire-beds. These beds were circular in form, eight feet in diameter, and about ten feet apart. The earth was burned hard for eight inches below the ashes. Under these beds were several human skeletons.

No. 1, a medium-sized adult, was extended on the back, head south, arms by the side. This was four feet below the centre of the northern fire-bed. No trace of a coffin was observed, but a rude hoe and a rough lance-head were at the left side.

No. 2 was four feet north of No. 1, at the same depth. It lay with the feet toward the centre of the mound, and was enclosed in a kind of coffin formed by leaning flat stones together over the body in the form of an inverted V, and placing a similar stone against the end at the head. A number of relics were with this skeleton, and on the stone at the head was a hematite celt. Two feet north of the head were the fragments of a large clay vessel.

No. 3, similarly placed, was four feet under the north edge of the other fire-bed. Some relics were found above the head, and others in a small conical vault near the left side.

No. 4, same depth as the preceding, had the head toward the centre of the mound. A small vault near the head contained several relics of different sorts.

Nos. 5 and 6 lay near together, with heads south. There as a small vault near the feet of the smaller skeleton.

None of these skeletons were found immediately in the centre of the mound, and all were about four feet below the natural surface of the ground, resting on the bottom of the pit, as were the little conical vaults. Nine vaults in addition to those mentioned were unearthed,—four of them on the bottom of the pit, and five above it. They were similar in form and size to those heretofore described. There was one toward the south side of the pit elongate in form, and not more than two feet wide and two feet high.

Another mound, numbered 30 in the original plat, had a circular pit beneath it, in which were several beehive-shaped clay vaults similar to those heretofore mentioned. The explorer, however, in this case, fails to mention the arrangement or to note particularly the contents, owing perhaps to the pit being partially filled with water, which prevented a thorough examination.

By a careful comparison of the discoveries made in the mounds of this Kanawha group with those made in the mounds of the Cherokee section, the reader will observe some striking similarities which cannot be easily accounted for upon any other theory than that of tribal identity or intimate relations of the peoples of the two sections. It is true that we find enclosures in the former locality, and none in the latter, and it is also true that we notice other dissimilarities; but some changes in customs and works are to be expected where there is a change of location. Necessities, materials, and environments are different, and bring about modifications of customs. These changes are apparent in all parts of the mound area, even where there are good reasons for attributing the works to the same people: in fact, they are sometimes found in a single group.

It is true, we cannot assert positively that the little conical clay vaults above described, except in one or two cases, were depositories of the dead, as were the conical bowlder vaults of North Carolina and East Tennessee; yet the very marked similarity in form and size, and correspondence in their arrangement in the tumuli, justify the belief that there was a relationship between the authors of the works of the two sections. Not only are they similar in size and form, but in both localities pits were dug in the original soil, the floor was covered with coals or ashes in some cases, and the vaults built on these and the mound heaped over them. It should also be borne in mind that vaults of this kind, arranged as here stated, have so far been found only in these two sections. The arrangement in a circle found in the mound in Sullivan County, Tenn., has its parallel in one of the mounds of the Kanawha group. In one was also found the pipe shown in Fig. 8; in the other, that shown in Fig. 5.

In further corroboration of the theory of relationship between the people of the two sections, may be mentioned the fact that in the mounds of both we find the peculiar basin-shaped beds placed in series one above another.

CHAPTER V.

HAVING traced back the tribe by the mound evidence thus far along the traditional line of migration with strong probability of being correct, we are prepared to take another backward step. As will be observed by the careful reader, reliance has been placed in this investigation upon what appear to be indications of peculiar customs. Connection with the group of which the great Grave Creek tumulus forms a prominent feature seems to be established, thus verifying the ancient "oration," or tradition, of which Haywood speaks. Allusion has also been made to the similarity, in some respects, of the works of the Kanawha group to those of Ohio, but there is more to be added on this point. Not only does it appear that it was a custom in both these sections to enclose the bodies of the dead in bark, to bury in wooden vaults, and to form at the bottom of mounds basin-shaped clay masses which have received the name "altars," but also to arrange wooden vaults the same way in the tumuli, and to build other structures similar to each other in form.

In confirmation of the statement in reference to the wooden vaults, attention is called to the description by Mr. H. L. Reynolds, in a recent bulletin of the Bureau of Ethnology, of a mound he explored in Paint Creek valley, Ohio.

This is the "square truncated mound" shown on No. 1, Plate XXI., "Ancient Monuments," which, by its close proximity to the combined square and circular enclosures known as the "Baum Works," is supposed to bear some intimate relation thereto.

As the description has been published, it is only necessary here to allude to such portions as have a bearing on the question before us.

At the time it was measured by Messrs. Squier and Davis it was a hundred and twenty-five feet in diameter, and fifteen feet in height. Since then its annual disturbance by plough and freshet has reduced the height to twelve feet, and increased the diameter to a hundred and forty. The same agencies have likewise destroyed its pyramidal form, so that now it resembles an upturned basin. It was composed, for the most part, of clay mottled with black loam, and in some places with patches of a grayish, plastic lime. The prominent feature is the evidence that two large wooden vaults, or structures of some kind, had been built here, one above the other, as in one of the Kanawha mounds heretofore described. Both of these structures had been built of upright posts, five inches in diameter and ten inches apart, forming a regular circle thirty six feet in diameter. The lower circle consisted of a single series, but the upper of two, eighteen inches apart, the outer series standing directly over the posts of the lower structure.

Separating the two structures was what the explorer terms "a thin, sagging streak of burnt clay," but which reminds us strongly of the basin-shaped clay beds found in the mounds of East Tennessee and Kanawha valley. Here and there upon its surface were traces of black wood-ashes and a small quantity of white bone-ashes. Horizontal timber moulds, smaller in size than the posts, filled, in places, with charcoal, could be seen distinctly lying against the inside of each line of posts. These appear to have been cross-beams or stays used for bracing-purposes. On the east side there was a break in each circle, of three feet two inches, in which there were no post-moulds. Within each circle, at different depths, and placed without any apparent regularity, were several skeletons Lying on the natural surface of the ground, running from the base of the lower series of posts toward the centre of the circle, were the remains of logs about eight inches in diameter. Directly over these timbers was a horizontal layer of decayed and burnt wood or bark, averaging half an inch thick. Notice should also be taken of the fact that this mound is on the lower level near the creek,—in fact, is one step or terrace below the bridge landing,—and is almost yearly surrounded by water from the overflow.

It is true that this mound shows some indication of being comparatively recent: in fact, Mr. Reynolds found in it a small piece of bone which he thought had been shaped with a steel knife. This supposition, if accepted, would seem to be incompatible with the theory that attributes works of this type to the Cherokees. We give the data, however, as they are, and will present our explanation further on.

We observe in this mound the somewhat unusual arrangement of one wooden structure above another, seen elsewhere only in the Kanawha and Grave Creek groups; we also notice that in each case the walls of these structures are formed by standing the timbers upright. There is, however, one particular worthy of note, in which those of the Ohio mound differ from the others; to wit, the much larger size of the former, suggesting the possibility that they were councilhouses, and not vaults. But should this conclusion be adopted, we find parallels in the customs of the Cherokees and mound-builders of the Cherokee district.

Mr. Lucien Carr of Cambridge, Mass., explored a mound in Lee County, Va., in which were found indications of a large circular or oval wooden structure. From his description, as given in the "Tenth Annual Report of the Peabody Museum," we take the following extract:—

"The mound in question, a truncated oval in shape, stands alone on a gentle slope; and, having been in cultivation for many years, the wear and tear of the plough and the gradual weathering-away of the summit made it impossible to get at its exact measurements. A careful examination, however, showed it to be about three hundred feet in circumference at the base, and nineteen feet in height. . . . On the top was a level space, oval in shape, the diameters being respectively about fifteen and forty feet. At a distance of eight or ten feet from the brow of the mound, on the slope, there were found buried in the earth the decaying stumps of a series of cedar-posts, which, I was informed by Mr. Ely, at one time completely encircled it. He also told me that at every ploughing he struck more or less of these posts, and, on digging for them, some six or seven were found at different places, and in such order as showed that they had been placed in the earth at regular intervals and according to a definite plan. On the top, in the line of the greatest diameter, and near the centre of the mound, another and larger post or column, also of cedar, was found. . . . The location and regularity of these posts, and their position with reference to the central column, would seem to show that the summit of the mound at one time had been occupied by some sort of a building, possibly a rotunda or council-chamber, as the ground plan answers to the description of one which Bartram found in the town of Cowe on the 'Tanase' River among the Cherokees, the very people who formerly held all this section of country."

In the mound, and within the circle of posts, several skeletons were found placed irregularly and at different depths, as in the case of the mound opened by Mr. Reynolds. Mr. Carr further remarks that "there were found scattered about everywhere, throughout the whole of the upper half of the excavation, in different places and at various depths, beds of ashes, burnt earth, and charcoal,—usually cedar or chestnut,—sometimes one above and overlapping the other, with an intervening stratum of earth of greater or less thickness."

This is an important and interesting fact in comparing the works of the different sections alluded to.

Indications of similar structures were found in some three or four mounds explored by the Bureau assistants in East Tennessee. In one case the series of posts was found at considerable depth, showing that earth had been added subsequent to its erection.

Adair says that "every town has a large edifice which with propriety may be called the mountain house in comparison of those already described. But the only difference between it and the winter house or stove is in its dimensions and application. It is usually built on the top of a hill, and in that separate and imperial state-house the old beloved men and head warriors meet on material business, or to divert themselves and feast and dance with the rest of the people."

The winter houses referred to were, according to his statement, made as follows: a sufficient number of strong, forked posts were fixed deep in the ground "at a proportional distance, in a circular form, all of an equal height, about five or six feet above the surface of the ground; above these they tie large pieces of the heart of white oak. . . . In the middle of the fabric they fix very deep in the ground four large pine posts in a quadrangular form."

According to Mr. Mooney,—who has furnished the writer with some particulars on the subject in addition to what are found in his paper heretofore mentioned,—on account of the sanctity attached to the location in the minds of the people, a new town-house was usually built upon the site of the old one. The Cherokee town-houses were necessarily located in the immediate vicinity of a stream, and where there was about it a level area. The reasons for this were (1) that the dances were held around and about these public houses, frequently beginning inside, and ending on the level area around them; and (2) ceremonial bathing formed an important part of the proceedings connected with their sacred dances, such as the green-corn dance and the medicine dance, where the whole body of the performers came out of the town-house to the water, and, after certain ablutions, returned thereto. It was necessary, therefore, that the building should be near a stream. As the level areas in their narrow mountain valleys are often overflowed, it is quite probable that in order to place these sacred houses above the floods, they were, as stated in tradition, located on artificial mounds. "Moreover," adds Mr. Mooney, "the town-house was the depository of numerous ceremonial objects which could not readily be removed in a sudden emergency. And, as it is said traditionally that a sacred fire was kept burning on a peculiar hearth excavated in the centre of the earthen floor, this could not be removed from the hearth-place, and hence some provision for its protection was necessary."

Whatever may be the opinion entertained in regard to the relation of the mound-builders of the different sections to each other, or be thought of Mr. Mooney's suggestions, it must be admitted that the above statement gives a satisfactory reason for placing the pyramidal mound of the Baum Works, Ohio, on the lower level near the creek, rather than on the higher level occupied by the square and circle.

In confirmation of Mr. Mooney's statement, we find the following in Adair's "History." Speaking of the Cherokees, he says, "Their towns are always close to some river or creek, as there the land is commonly very level and fertile, on account of the frequent washings off the mountains, and the moisture it receives from the waters that run through their fields. And such a situation enables them to perform the ablutions connected with their religious worship."

Another respect in which the Kanawha works resemble those of Ohio is the presence among them of enclosures, some of which are approximately true circles. There is also among the former a true "hill-fort," located on the top of a bold and partially isolated headland, overlooking the valley for some miles up and down the river.

We have now, as before stated, travelled back along the path of migration to the Ohio region, the mound testimony agreeing substantially at every step with the traditions. As we now enter a well-known field which has been somewhat thoroughly cultivated by archæologists, and which is considered, in the minds of many antiquarians, sacred ground, we are aware that we must move with cautious steps, as any attempt to bring forward a new theory in regard to the ancient works of this region is attended with more than ordinary risk. It will therefore be appropriate to introduce at this point some general considerations which have a bearing on the questions at issue.

One result of the more recent explorations and study of the ancient works of the mound region is the conviction that the mound-builders were divided into numerous tribes, though belonging substantially to the same culture state, which was of a lower grade than that attained by the people of Mexico and Central America, and apparently somewhat less advanced than that of the Pueblo tribes of New Mexico and Arizona. However, there are no data to justify the belief that they pertained to different "races," using this term in its broad and legitimate sense. This assertion will, of course, be questioned by some of our archæologists who base their conclusions in reference to this subject on the forms of the skulls. Without entering into a discussion of this question, which would draw too heavily on our space, and is not appropriate at this point, it may be asserted, with the assurance of being sustained by the facts, that the study of the forms of mound-builders' skulls has not been productive of any satisfactory results bearing upon the question of races or nationality. This is shown by the remarks of Mr. Lucien Carr, in his paper on the "Crania from Stone Graves in Tennessee," published in the "Eleventh Annual Report of the Peabody Museum:"—

"Names, however, are of but little import: the one central fact is to be found in the presence in these graves of skulls, which, after excluding those tabulated as distorted or much flattened, are shown by their measurements to belong to the two extremes of classification, and which cannot be brought into the same group without doing violence to all ideas of craniology. If the terms 'dolichocephalism' and 'brachycephalism' mean any thing, then these two forms of skulls are to be found here, and there is no method of measurement sufficiently elastic to include them both under one head. This fact is by no means new or novel, though it has not been many years since Dr. Morton and anthropologists of his school stoutly maintained the uniform brachycephalic type of crania among all the American aborigines except the Eskimo. Of late years, however, the contrary opinion, so ably advocated by Dr. D. Wilson, has been steadily gaining ground, and to-day there is little hazard in saying that it is generally received. But the evidence furnished by this collection seems to lead still farther; and we are required not only to admit the existence of different forms of skulls, as there well might be in different tribes, but also to conclude that they are to be found among the same people or peoples living under the same tribal organization, much after the fashion in which they are to-day known to exist among the composite peoples of our great commercial cities. This is hardly in accord with the opinion generally held as to the purity of race in prehistoric times; but it seems impossible to avoid the conclusion, if it be admitted that the fact that these skulls were found buried together indiscriminately in the same style or set of graves in the same mound, and so far as we can judge at or near the same time, is any proof that they belonged to people of the same tribe and race."

It will be seen from this conclusion of one best qualified to express an opinion on this subject, that a classification of the mound-builders upon the forms of the skulls is not only unsatisfactory, but is misleading and valueless. That the people found inhabiting the continent at the time of the Columbian discovery may have been, and probably were, derived from different races, is not denied. Possibly the mound-builders of the section herein designated the "mound region" may have been derived from different races; but, if so, this cannot be determined by the crania found in the mounds of the Mississippi valley. Indications of tribal peculiarities, of variations in local customs depending on environment, and perhaps traces even of customs peculiar to certain stocks or families, are observed in the ancient works of the region indicated, but nothing whatever to suggest different races. This is a bold and venturous statement to make, in view of what has been published on this subject; nevertheless the writer feels justified in making it, and believes that the data, when thoroughly studied, will sustain him.

The evidence of division into tribes is found in the numerous indications of intertribal warfare, such as the works of defence of various kinds met with in different sections. For instance, there are the hill-forts of Ohio, of which Fort Ancient is a well-known example. No one has ever doubted that these were constructed for defence. Nor is it likely the other enclosures, such as the circles, squares, and octagons, would have been ascribed to any other object but for the introduction of the theory of a semi-civilized, mound-building race, with its priesthood and religious ceremonies. Assume that the authors were the ancestors of the Indian tribes found inhabiting the country, and the idea of this overpowering religious influence vanishes at once. The enclosures of New York, Michigan, Kentucky, Tennessee, south eastern Missouri, and the Gulf States, are admitted to be defensive works. In addition to these, there are in many places defensive walls and embankments across projecting spurs, peninsulas, and river bends. Village sites are also often found in positions which could have been selected for no conceivable reason except that they might be easily defended against attack.

The only reasonable explanation of these facts, and of the evidences of different customs found in the mounds, is that the mound-builders consisted of different tribes. Even in the comparatively limited area of Ohio are found abundant evidences of the presence of different tribes, and of successive occupation by different peoples. The same thing is true also of the areas embraced in eastern Iowa, Wisconsin, Illinois, Indiana, and Kentucky; but, on the other hand, western New York, a strip along the lake border of Ohio, and the Cherokee region of East Tennessee and western North Carolina, appear to be exceptions to this rule.

CHAPTER VI.

As the connection indicated between the works of the Kanawha valley and those of Ohio relates primarily to the sepulchral and so-called "sacrificial mounds," and secondarily to the geometric enclosures of the type found in the Scioto valley, attention is called to the latter.

Forty years ago, Messrs. Squier and Davis, while admitting that some of the enclosures of this State were built for defence, advanced the theory that a large number of the earth-works were designed for sacred or religious purposes, and places for performing superstitious rites,—a view which has generally been adopted by subsequent writers. That this theory was based upon a preconceived notion held by these authors, is apparent from the following statement in "Ancient Monuments:" "We have reason to believe that the religious system of the mound-builders, like that of the Aztecs, exercised among them a great, if not a controlling, influence. Their government may have been, for aught we know, a government of the priesthood,—one in which the priestly and civil functions were jointly exercised, and one sufficiently powerful to have secured in the Mississippi valley, as it did in Mexico, the erection of many of those vast monuments which for ages will continue to challenge the wonder of men."

Dr. Daniel Wilson not only takes the same view in his "Prehistoric Man," but expands and emphasizes it. He even goes so far as to assert that the earth-works of the Iroquois present, in some respects, a greater contrast to those of the mound-builders (of Ohio) than the latter do to the elaborate architecture of Mexico and Yucatan. "They form groups," he continues, "of symmetrical enclosures, square, circular, elliptical, and octagonal, with long connecting avenues suggesting comparisons with the British Avebury, or the Hebridean Callernish; with the Breton Carnac, or even with the temples and sphinx avenues of the Egyptian Karnak and Luxor."

If we lay aside all preconceived notions of a highly cultured race of mound-builders with a priestly hierarchy, and study these remains in the light of such data as we possess, instead of looking at them through the halo of a finely wrought theory, the inappropriateness of such comparisons becomes apparent. What shall we say of the attempt to compare the dirt walls of these groups of combined circles and squares with the great temple of Karnak, termed by Fergusson "the noblest effort of architectural magnificence ever produced by the hand of man"? of likening the simple earthen parallels, thrown up perhaps with wooden spades, to the avenue of crio sphinxes, and the magnificent, columned hall of the Egyptian temple? In what respect do these earth-works of the mound-builders resemble the palace at Palenque, or Casa del Gobernador and House of the Nuns at Uxmal? It is only necessary to put the question: the reply is self-evident. Yet the writer just quoted, who may be taken as the leading representative of the school to which he belongs, sees, in some respects, less contrast between these two classes of structures than between the earth-works of the Iroquois and those of the mound-builders of Ohio.

Omitting, perhaps, a dozen geometrical works, the enclosures of Ohio, New York, and other sections, are admitted to be for defensive purposes, and are of a character conformable to savage life. And in reply to Dr. Wilson it may be truly affirmed, that if we compare the larger work on Plate XIX. of "Ancient Monuments"—which is in the immediate vicinity of the celebrated "Mound City," Ross County, O.— with that on Plate II. of Squier's "Aboriginal Monuments of New York," the similarity is so marked (except in size) that one might be substituted for the other without bringing into, or omitting from, the former group any important character. Yet here is what was considered by the authors of "Ancient Monuments" pre-eminently the sacred or religious city of the Ohio mound-builders; and, what is worthy of mention, the accompanying enclosure, so like that of New York, has a central mound, which was examined by Messrs. Squier and Davis, and pronounced by them "clearly a place of sacrifice."

A number of such general resemblances between the works of the two sections could be pointed out; yet it is admitted that the two classes of remains bear evidence of being the works of different tribes, but not of different races, or of peoples in such widely different culture states as to justify Dr. Wilson's extravagant statement.

The complicated group, consisting of circles, a square, octagon, and parallels, at Newark is unquestionably the most noted, as well as the most extensive, of its class in the mound section. As these cover an area estimated at two miles square, what, it may well be asked, must be the estimate of the size and population of the village that required such an extensive system of works devoted to religious services and superstitious rites? The great circle at Avebury, England, the most extensive of the so-called druidical structures of Europe, embraces only about thirty-six acres; while here is an octagon enclosing fifty acres, one circle including twenty, another thirty, and a square embracing twenty acres. The race-track, buildings, and other appurtenances of the Fair

Association of a county containing probably a hundred thousand inhabitants are enclosed in a single one of these circles. If these were but places where games were held and religious ceremonies performed, where are we to find the indications of the immense village that required such vast amphitheatres?

It is remarkably strange that the mound-builders of central and southern Ohio alone, of all the ancient peoples of the mound region, should erect such extensive structures devoted to religious observances; that here alone the priestly influence should have been sufficiently powerful to produce such results. How is the development of this sacerdotal element in this limited area to be accounted for?

It is true that a few of these enclosures are remarkably correct geometrical figures, and present a puzzling question to the archæologist; but the usual explanation, that the authors were a people in a much higher state of culture than the Indians, serves but to increase the difficulty. On the one hand. it is only necessary to suppose that they were built for defence, and that the Indians of a certain tribe and era had learned the art of laying off correctly circles of large size, and the problem is solved. But, on the other hand, the supposition of a highly cultured race, capable of forming these figures by means not within the reach or capacity of the more advanced Indians, introduces a host of still more troublesome questions. That the ancient works of the Southern States and of New York are to be ascribed to the Indians, is too clearly established by historical and other evidence to be longer denied; and it is even admitted, that associated with the prehistoric monuments of the valleys of the Muskingum, the Scioto, Brush Creek, the Little Miami and Big Miami, are mounds and works of later times, some of which were made by the historic tribes or their immediate ancestors. Notwithstanding this supposition of a much earlier occupation by a veritable mound-building people of advanced culture, there are works here ascribed to this people which present no indications of greater age than some of those attributed to Indians. How is this to be accounted for on the latter theory?

The fact, well known to all archæologists, that minor works of art are found in these typical monuments of the same character as those obtained from mounds attributable to the Indians, presents another question difficult to answer on this theory. The "Monitor" pipe, or pipe with broad base running out in front and behind the bowl, is considered typical of the people who built the "sacrificial mounds" and "sacred enclosures" of Ohio; yet, according to Adair, the Cherokees made pipes of precisely this pattern, as he says "the fore part of each commonly runs out with a sharp peak, two or three fingers broad and a quarter of an inch thick, on both sides of the bowl lengthwise; they cut several pictures with a great deal of skill and labour." This seems not only to connect the builders of these typical Ohio works with the Indians, thus presenting a difficult problem for the advocates of the above theory to solve, but forms another strong link in the chain of Cherokee history we are trying to follow. There are other difficulties in the way of this hypothesis which our limited space will not permit us to present. There are other questions, however, relating to these enclosures, which require notice here, as they have some bearing on the theory advanced in this paper, and must affect to some extent the conclusions reached.

It is believed that the evidence presented will be accepted as sufficient to justify the supposition that the Tallegwi of tradition must be identified with the Cherokees, and that they formerly lived in the Ohio valley. Having shown that the people of this tribe built mounds in their historic seat, and were in all probability the authors of the Kanawha and Grave Creek works, it is reasonable to conclude that they built mounds and constructed other works during their residence in Ohio. If this be admitted, their identification with the Tallegwi would indicate that, during their long contest with the Delawares and Huron-Iroquois, they built defensive works, as it is stated in Heckewelder's version of the tradition, that "the enemy [the Tallegwi] fortified their large towns and erected fortifications, especially on large rivers and near lakes, where they were successively attacked, and sometimes by the allies" (the Delawares and Iroquois). Although it is to be presumed that this is somewhat colored to conform to the interpretation of the narrator or author, there can be little doubt that the Tallegwi erected defensive structures in order to resist their enemies. This is probably implied in the Walam-Olum, where it is stated that "the Talega towns were too strong."

If the enclosures are defensive works, they present nothing incompatible with the theory herein advanced, but rather tend to confirm it. Even supposing they were intended for sacred or superstitious uses, they must have been constructed for the purpose of defending the gathered assemblies from sudden attack by enemies. Take, for example, the Baum Works shown in Fig. 1, Plate XIX., of the "Ancient Monuments," and copied in our Fig. 9. For what purpose were the walls built, except for defence? Is it to be supposed that they were intended solely as sitting-places for the spectators? Those around the square alone would have seated eight or ten thousand persons, and the wall of the circle as many more; yet the remains present no indications of an extensive village. We may also ask, with good reason, why one enclosure was square and the other circular, when the builders must have known that the latter afforded the better chance of observing the ceremonies. Are we to assume that different enclosures were made for the different kinds of rites and games? The only reasonable conclusion, even under the supposition that these were "tabooed" or sacred places, is, that the walls were built for defence, and, as Atwood judged from his discoveries, were stockaded. But this brings up the inquiry, "Why were the sacred grounds enclosed, while the village remained without defensive walls?"

Although it is not probable that all the mystery connected with these structures will be explained away, yet the sup-

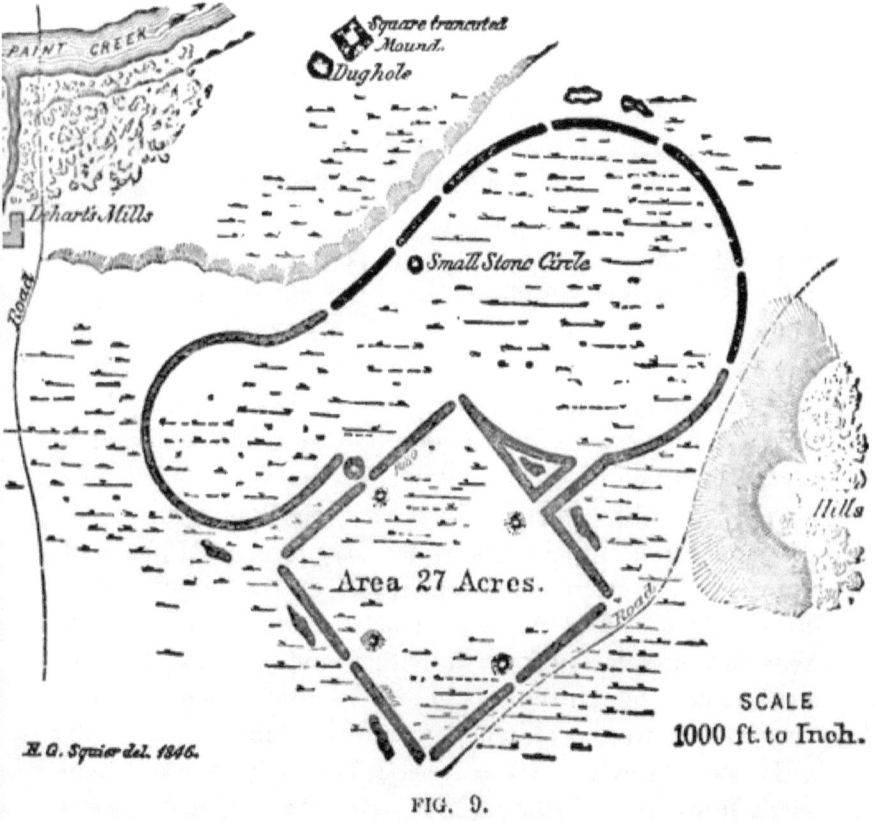

FIG. 9.

position that they were defensive works of people in the same culture grade as the Indians simplifies the problem, and enables us to present at least a partial explanation which is consistent with other data susceptible of interpretation.

Referring again to the Baum group shown in the figure, what is more likely than that the square enclosed the village, and the circle the maize-field? On the pyramidal mound was the council-house, within and around which the ceremonial dances were held; and near by was the creek in which the ablutions were performed. The council-house in this case was not in the village; the latter being built near the hills, contiguous to cool springs of water, thus rendering the distance from it to the creek too great for the convenience of the bathers. The writer is aware that this explanation will not apply in full to all the enclosures of this type, as the conditions are not the same in all the localities; and it is more than likely that the customs of the villages varied to some extent, although pertaining to the same tribe. The probable differences in the age of the villages, and the modifications of customs, are also to be taken into consideration; nevertheless this supposition gives us a key that will unlock most of the mystery of these works. They are in most cases located near a stream, and consist of a square or octagon with its gateways and protecting mounds surrounding the village, and a circle enclosing the corn-field. As a rule, the small circles, which may have been places of amusement and ceremony, are outside of the large enclosures. Even at Fort Ancient, which no one doubts is a defensive work, the supposed race-track and principal mounds are outside, though the crescent, in front of which the ceremonial rites were performed, is within the fort.

In some cases, as at the Liberty Township Works ("Ancient Monuments," Plate XX.), a special arrangement seems to have been made for this purpose. Here we see a connected third circle, much smaller than the other two, in which is a crescent and mound; there is, however, a little exterior circle. We notice here that the square or village site is near the bluff from whence springs issue.

The square of the Seip Works ("Ancient Monuments,"

No. 2, Plate XXI.) and of that figured in No. 3 (same plate) are next the stream, as there were no springs in reach.

The complicated group at Newark, of course, presents features difficult to explain; but it is apparent that there were two villages, probably established at different times, but both occupied from the time the latter was built until the whole was abandoned. The octagon is near the creek, but its position was doubtless selected on account of the spring near its northern corner. The southern circle, E, was possibly a place devoted chiefly to ceremonies and games. One line of parallels seems to have been a passageway from one village to another. It is apparent from their courses and the topographical features of the area that none of these guarded ways were intended for race-tracks. That the small, circular enclosure F, known as the "Observatory Circle," was not sufficient in extent to supply the villages with bread, is admitted: hence it was necessary to assume that there were unenclosed fields, probably on the land north of the group, between the parallels running east and west, and in the area east of the pond. It is possible that the space between the two lines of parallels, running east and west, was partially occupied by dwellings, especially that portion on the upper, level land. These suggestions are of course largely speculative; nevertheless, if there be any truth in the tradition of the Tallegwi, it is probable that here they made their first determined stand after defeat in open battle. The people of other villages, not enclosed, probably fled thither, and joined in erecting fortifications and defensive walls. Be this as it may, it is apparent that they belong to the same type as those in the Scioto and Paint Creek valleys, and may be ascribed to the people who built the latter. That they were defensive seems to be established by the considerations presented, and others which might be urged did space allow us to offer them. It is apparent to any one not biassed by a preconceived theory, who will study these works carefully, that their characteristics are essentially aboriginal: in other words, there is nothing in their form or construction contradictory to the theory of their Indian origin, except it be the single fact that a few of them approach very nearly to true geometrical figures. That it was a custom among the Indians north and south to build circular enclosures and forts, is fully attested by the historical records; it is also known that some of the Indian forts in the northern section were polygonal, especially those built by the Iroquois tribes. Numerous instances can be cited where villages were surrounded by fortifications in both these forms.

The suggestion that the circles adjoining squares were built around maize-fields is not original with the writer, as it had already been presented by Lewis H. Morgan, in his " Houses and House Life of the American Aborigines." He remarks, that " with respect to the large circular enclosures, adjacent to and communicating with the squares, it is not necessary that we should know their object. The one attached to the High Bank Pueblo contains twenty acres of land, and doubtless subserved some useful purpose in their plan of life. The first suggestion which presents itself is, that as a substitute for a fence it surrounded the garden of the village in which they cultivated their maize, beans, squashes, and tobacco. At the Minnitaree village a similar enclosure may now be seen by the side of the village, surrounding their cultivated land, consisting partly of hedge and partly of stakes." Whether these dirt walls were mere supports to stockades is a question not yet settled; nevertheless it is probable they were surmounted by stakes, or supported a wooden fence or screen of some kind. The fact that the ditch is here usually on the inside cuts but little figure in the discussion, as we find this to be the case in many works which are undoubtedly of a defensive character, as Fort Ancient, and the circular enclosure in Iowa shown in Plate II., "Fifth Annual Report of the Bureau of Ethnology." In fact, this was consistent with the Indian mode of warfare. Long tells us, in the account of his expedition, that sometimes they would hastily dig a trench, throwing the dirt on the danger side, and thus form a defensive barrier.

Whether the hill-forts are to be attributed to the authors of the circles and squares is doubtful: in fact, the indications appear to lead to the opposite conclusion. Certainly there is no reason for supposing that Fort Ancient, Fortified Hill, and other works of this character in the Miami valleys, were built by this people. The writer is inclined to the belief that they are the work of the Shawnees, but cannot undertake at this time to give his reasons for this opinion.

As the so called "altars" form a link in this historic chain, we may as well remark here that the names "sacrificial mounds" and "altars," implying human sacrifice, have been brought into use without even the shadow of evidence therefor. As Morgan has truly observed, "there is no propriety in the use of either of these terms, or in the conclusions they would force us to adopt. . . . These clay beds were not adapted to the barbarous work." Possibly they may have been places where prisoners were burned, which was the chief sacrifice offered by Indians. The basin-shaped clay beds of the Kanawha and East Tennessee mounds seem to have grown out of them, and their uses were probably similar.

CHAPTER VII.

THE close agreement between the testimony of the mounds and the traditions of both Cherokees and Delawares is somewhat remarkable, and justifies us in believing that they have a basis of truth. We are at least warranted in accepting the theory that the first-named people formerly dwelt in Ohio, and built some of the noted monuments of that State. The number and character of the defensive works indicate that there was a long contest and an obstinate resistance on the part of the original inhabitants. The geographical position of these works makes it apparent, as has often been remarked by writers on this subject, that there was a pressure by northern hordes which finally resulted in driving the inhabitants of the fertile valleys of the Scioto and Muskingum southward. Some of these writers take it for granted that they fled through Kentucky and Tennessee into the Gulf States, and became incorporated with the tribes of that section. If this be assumed as correct, it only tends to confirm the theory of an Indian origin.

A study, however, of the pipes alone, makes it evident that this conclusion cannot be maintained. That the mound-builders of Ohio made and used pipes is proven by the large number found in the tumuli, and that they cultivated tobacco may reasonably be inferred from this fact. Although varied indefinitely by the addition of animal and other figures, the typical or simple form in use among them appears to have been that known at present as the "Monitor" pipe, shown in Fig. 68, "Ancient Monuments," and Fig. 177, Rau's "Archæological Collection of the National Museum." The peculiar feature is the broad, flat, and slightly curved base or stem, which projects in front of the bowl to an extent equal to the perforated end. This form is so peculiar that it must be considered ethnic or local. However, as will be seen by reference to the "Proceedings of the Davenport Academy of Natural Sciences" and the "Smithsonian Re-

FIG. 10.

port for 1882," it is found in eastern Iowa and northern Illinois, and appears to be the only form found in that region: hence it cannot be considered local.

Now, it is somewhat remarkable that nearly all the pipes of this form and the modifications thereof, ending in the modern form shown in Fig. 6, are found in a belt commencing in eastern Iowa, running thence through northern Illinois, eastern Indiana, southern Ohio, and thence bending south through Kanawha valley, and ending in western North Carolina. The first modification is seen in Fig. 8, and found in Ohio, the Kanawha valley, and North Carolina; the second, shown in Fig. 10, is found in Ohio and the

Cherokee district; the third, shown in Fig. 5, is found in East Tennessee; and the last, shown in Fig. 6, is found in the North Carolina mounds.

Although specimens, chiefly of the first modification, have been discovered in New York and Massachusetts, it is not known that the "Monitor" or any of its manifest modifications prevailed, or was even in use, at any point south of the belt mentioned. Pipes in the form of birds and other animals are not uncommon, as may be seen by reference to Plate XXIII. of Jones's "Antiquities of the Southern Indians;" but the platform is a feature wholly unknown in the Gulf States or middle Tennessee, as are also the derivatives from it.

This fact stands in direct opposition to the theory that the mound-builders of Ohio fled southward across Kentucky and Tennessee, and became incorporated with the tribes of the Southern States, as it is scarcely possible that such sturdy smokers as they must have been, would have abandoned all at once their favorite pipe. The change, as it was in the other direction, would have been gradual. This evidence, however, has a very significant bearing on another point; for, if the testimony introduced justifies the theory advanced in this paper, then it is probable the Cherokees entered the immediate valley of the Mississippi from the north-west, striking it in the region of Iowa. This supposition is strongly corroborated, not only by the presence of the "Monitor" pipe and its derivatives along the belt designated, but also by the structure and contents of many of the mounds found along the Mississippi in the region of eastern Iowa and western Illinois. So striking is this resemblance, that it has been remarked by explorers whose opinions could not have been biassed by this theory.

Mr. William McAdams, in an address to the American Association for the Advancement of Science, remarks that "mounds such as are here described, in the American bottoms and low lands of Illinois, are seldom found on the bluffs. On the rich bottom-lands of the Illinois River, within fifty miles of its mouth, I have seen great numbers of them, and examined several. The people who built them were probably connected with the Ohio mound-builders, although in this vicinity they seem not to have many earthen embankments or walls enclosing areas of land, as is common in Ohio. Their manner of burial was similar to the Ohio mound-builders, however, and in this particular they had customs similar to mound-builders of Europe." Two mounds in Calhoun County, Ill., one of which was opened by Mr. McAdams and the other by one of the Bureau assistants, presented the clay mass in the regular form of the Ohio "altar." But what is strange, though not without parallel, is the fact that we find the structure and contents of some of the eastern Iowa mounds similar to what is seen in the Cherokee district of North Carolina and East Tennessee. Here, among other things, are seen the cubical piles or "altars" of unhewn stone with bones about them, precisely as found in some of the North Carolina burial-places, pottery bearing a strong resemblance to that of Ohio, and mounds with stone strata. A mound in Franklin County, Ind., described and figured by Mr. Homsher in the "Smithsonian Report for 1882," presents features strongly resembling those observed in tumuli attributed to the Cherokees. Here we see the rectangular heaps of cobblestones like those in the North Carolina mounds, and stratification and arrangement of skeletons as in the East Tennessee mounds, also the stone stratum observed in the Iowa works.

Having now traced the tribe back to the western boundary of the mound region, we are prepared to take a glance downward along the line of migration, bridging by deduction such breaks as appear in the testimony.

According to the data presented, we find them first on the west bank of the Mississippi, a tribe of comparatively limited numbers, slowly extending their settlements or shifting up or down the stream between the mouth of the Des Moines River and what is now the northern boundary of Iowa. If we may judge by their works, it would seem that it was necessary only at this northern point of their extension to fortify against enemies. A suggestion as to who these enemies were will be offered a little further on. It is impossible to give any satisfactory estimate of the length of time they occupied this locality; it was long enough, however, for them to acquire certain peculiar customs, some of which were not wholly dropped until they came into contact with the whites many centuries later. It is possible that here they began to build mounds, but explorations westward of this area have not been carried on to a sufficient extent to speak with certainty on this point. It was here, no doubt, that the platform pipe with animal figures came into use. The ornamentation of their pottery, and the forms of their vessels, suggest the possibility of contact or intercourse with southern mound-building tribes. There is also abundance of evidence that they had acquired the art of manufacturing cloth, and were acquainted with copper. The evident admixture, however, in these mounds, by intrusive burial, of articles of more recent times with those of the original burials, renders it somewhat difficult to decide positively as to the advance made in art by this people while residing in this locality.

After passing to the east side of the river, it appears that they moved some distance farther to the south, their utmost limits in this direction being in Calhoun County, Ill. The reason for this may have been the presence of the same enemies who opposed their northward movement on the opposite side of the river. Of course, without the knowledge of all the mound testimony, any attempt to descend into details of the movements of the tribe would carry us wholly into the realms of speculation.

All that the mounds teach us in regard thereto is the extent of the area occupied, and the encroachments of works of other types which may or may not be contemporaneous.

It is a fact perhaps worthy of notice, that, while the remains of the effigy-builders on the west side of the river reach but little south of the fortified point before alluded to, they are found on the Illinois side as far south as the latitude of Peoria.

Passing on eastward, we next find indications of their presence in eastern Indiana, whence it seems they gradually moved into central Ohio, finding, as we judge from some works along the southern border of their line of migration, some opposition. Their stay in this attractive region must have been long, and for most of the time a period of peace. The reasons for this conclusion are, first, the indications of the growth of the tribe, judging by the number of works and the statements in the Delaware tradition, which imply that it had spread northward near to the lakes; and, second, the localities of the defensive works, which indicate that their chief contest was with a northern foe. If the latter supposition be correct, it would seem to imply that until this contest they had not found it necessary to build defensive structures.

These, of course, are speculations, and only advanced as such; but there is one thing in relation to their removal from this region for which there appears to be historical, traditional, and mound testimony, and which has some bearing on the preceding suggestions. This is, that their departure was in separate bodies, and at intervals of considerable length.

That some were in their historic seat before the time of De Soto's expedition, and possibly as early as the thirteenth century, has been shown. On the other hand, we have the statement of Bishop Ettwein, in a communication made to Gen. Washington, that the last of them did not remove from the region of Ohio until about the year 1700. We also find in the mounds of Ohio indications of intercourse with people residing in the mountain region of North Carolina.

It has been objected, with some show of reason, that the theory advanced in this paper cannot be correct, because there are no such enclosures in North Carolina and East Tennessee as those in Ohio, because no true "Monitor" pipes have been found in the mountain section, and because no engraved shells have been found in the Ohio mounds. The first of these objections has already been alluded to; but we may add, that this people found themselves able, in their mountain fastnesses, to protect themselves against all their Indian foes without erecting artificial defences. The second objection, as we have already shown, is answered by a somewhat remarkable historical statement by Adair. When he speaks of pipes "full a span long, with the fore part commonly running out with a short peak, two or three fingers broad and a quarter of an inch thick, *on both sides of the bowl lengthwise,*" he can refer to no other known pipe than the "Monitor," or the very slightly modified form with straight base, found also in the Ohio mounds. As the author quoted wrote before any specimens had been unearthed from mounds, he must have seen in use that of which he speaks. This, we repeat, is somewhat remarkable, and forms a link connecting the Cherokees and mound-builders of Ohio sufficient to warrant the theory here advanced, were there no other evidences bearing on the question.

The fact that no engraved shells bearing designs like those found in North Carolina and Tennessee have been discovered in Ohio forms no objection to the theory. Arts and customs are not always ethnical or tribal: some are acquired by contact and intercourse with other tribes. The custom of carving and wearing these shell gorgets did not originate with the Cherokees, but was acquired by contact with other tribes, after they had reached their southern home.

These objections do not militate against the theory, which is established on too broad a basis of facts and resemblances to be set aside by its failure to account for all the discoveries made. Investigations in regard to the origin and use of these ancient monuments must be made chiefly by comparisons and deductions, as historical evidence is in most cases wanting, and absolute demonstration impossible.

Attention was called in the first part of the paper to the conclusion reached by linguists, that the language of this tribe belongs to the Huron-Iroquois family, thus necessitating the inference that we must look to the same locality for the origin of both. This throws a faint ray of light on the history of our tribe preceding their arrival on the banks of the Mississippi. But before attempting to follow this slender clew, attention is called to some general considerations drawn from a comprehensive study of the monuments of the mound section.

In entering upon a discussion of the routes by which the mound-builders came into this section, an examination of the general distribution of the prehistoric remains is necessary. At present we are concerned only with what may be considered the boundaries thereof. Although the data are not sufficient to determine these limits accurately, enough has been ascertained to indicate what will probably be found in the end to be true.

Limiting the consideration to what are usually classed as the genuine works of the mound-builders, the eastern boundary extends from central New York along the Appalachian range to Virginia, diverging thence south-eastward so as to strike the Atlantic coast in South Carolina. The Gulf coast, west of Florida, appears to be generally bare of mounds (with the exception of shell and refuse heaps) for some distance toward the interior. On the north, the lakes and Rainy River form a tolerably well defined border, but west of the source of the Mississippi there is a northward extension into Manitoba which has not been fully traced; yet the indications are that but few ancient works will be discovered north of the Assiniboin region. Most of the mounds of this section which have been explored appear to be somewhat recent, though others bear evidence of being contemporaneous with the works of Wisconsin. On the west the plains appear to form the boundary from North Dakota to Texas, a line of recent works along the Missouri River forming the only exception, so far as known.

The statement frequently made, that the works of the mound-builders continue across Texas into Mexico, appears to be without any foundation; for up to the present time but few have been discovered south of Red River, except in the eastern part of Louisiana.

So far, therefore, as the facts ascertained are concerned, the distribution of the works of the mound-builders affords but little evidence on which to base a theory in regard to the lines along which the authors of these works entered the mound section. The exceptions, if any, are to be found in Florida and the North-west. But this statement must not be taken as indicative of a theory held by the writer, for he is not inclined to the opinion that the mound-building element, except possibly that of southern Florida, entered through this peninsula. Although he has reached no settled conclusion on this subject, he has been inclined to look more to the north-west and west for the lines of immigration than elsewhere, but freely confesses that he finds but little in the works along the border on which to base any theory.

While this is true considering the section as a whole in its relation to the other comprehensive archæological divisions of the continent, there are, on the other hand, decided indications of movements within the mound section.

The works of the effigy-mound district, confined chiefly to the southern half of Wisconsin and the immediately adjoining sections, are peculiar, and formed a puzzling factor to those holding the theory of one great nation of moundbuilders. The study of these appears to lead all those who have devoted attention to them to the conviction that the more elaborate forms, are, as a rule, older than the simpler ones.

Following up the slight clew thus afforded, and using the faint rays of light thrown on the history of the builders by the distribution of the mounds, we are led to believe that their entrance into the district was most likely at its southwestern corner, about what is now the north-eastern part of Iowa, and that the area longest occupied was the southwestern portion of Wisconsin. The indications are, that they shifted back and forth between the Mississippi River and Lake Michigan, and finally made their exit at the northwestern boundary of the State, a part going as far north as southern Manitoba. From there they at length passed southward into Dakota, where the mounds fade out, and the presence of the descendants of the builders — who, we are inclined to believe, pertain to the Dakotan stock — is indicated only by surface figures.

Another movement, traced by certain classes of works and vestiges of art which we ascribe to the ancestors of the Cherokees, was that already mentioned, extending from eastern Iowa through Illinois, Indiana, Ohio, and West Virginia, to the mountain region of North Carolina and East Tennessee.

A third line is indicated by certain types of prehistoric remains extending from Michigan, along the southern shore of Lake Erie, into New York; but nothing has been found in these remains by which to determine the direction of the movement. There is little doubt, however, that the works along this line are attributable to one or more tribes of the Huron-Iroquois family.

Another class of works forms an irregular line extending from southern Illinois, through Kentucky and middle Tennessee, to the north-east corner of Georgia; the area of chief occupation, and position of longest quietude, being that portion of the Cumberland valley in middle Tennessee. The works along this belt, which we attribute to the Shawnees, consist chiefly of stone graves of a particular type, and mounds; they fail, however, to give any satisfactory evidence as to the direction of the movement. Nevertheless there are, along portions of the line, some evidences of a shifting back and forth; and the minor vestiges of art prove beyond question that the authors were contemporaneous with the builders of the mounds of East Tennessee and North Carolina.

Although the banks of the Mississippi are lined with prehistoric monuments from Lake Pepin to the mouth of Red River, showing that this was a favorite section to the ancient inhabitants, yet a study of these remains does not give support to the theory that this great water highway was a line of migration during the mound-building age, except for short distances. It was, no doubt, a highway of traffic and war-parties, but the movements of tribes were across rather than up and down it. We do not assert this as a theory or simple deduction, but as a fact proven by the mounds, whatever may be the theory in regard to their origin or uses. The longest stretch, where those apparently the work of one people are found on one bank, is that from Dubuque to the mouth of the Des Moines. As we move up and down, we find repeated changes from one type to another. In addition to this, are the intermingling of other types, and indications in most places of successive occupation by different tribes. It is a very natural supposition that the people first reaching the bank of this broad stream, or of any of the other large streams of our country, would continue their course along it, but the mounds give no support to the theory.

A study of this subject ought to lead us to the proper conclusion, for it is evident that the natural condition of a mound-building people is one of permanency: hence their movements are governed largely by pressure from other tribes, and not by choice. No evidence has yet been found in the mounds pointing to the first comers into the section. On the contrary, all the evidences of migration point at the same time to pressure or obstacles in one or more directions. For example: the mound-builders of Wisconsin must have found some obstacle which prevented them from continuing their course eastward around the southern end of Lake Michigan, while the pressure which drove them from the area they had occupied so long seems to have come from the north-east.

The singular course of the people who buried in the stone graves south of the Ohio, whether moving eastward or westward, can be explained only on the theory of the presence of other tribes to the north and south; and this is probably true, as has been suggested, in regard to the people who travelled from eastern Iowa to Ohio.

Indications of movements are found in other portions of the mound section, but those mentioned are all which have any immediate bearing on the subject under consideration at present.

Returning now to the point where we paused in our journey backward along the pathway of the Cherokees, the inquiry arises, "From what point, or along what line, did they come to their halting-place on the banks of the Mississippi?" As has already been stated, it is now conceded by linguists that their language is an offshoot of the Huron-Iroquois family,—a relationship long ago surmised by Dr. Barton and Mr. Gallatin. We may therefore, in answer to the above inquiry, though in a somewhat broader sense than given, adopt the language of Mr. Horatio Hale in speaking of the more closely allied branches of this family: "There can be no doubt that their ancestors formed one body, and indeed dwelt at one time (as has been well said of the an cestors of the Indo-European populations), under one roof. There was a Huron-Iroquois 'family pair' from which all these tribes were descended. In what part of the world this ancestral household resided is a question which admits of no reply except from the merest conjecture." He adds, however, "that the evidence of language, so far as it has yet been examined, seems to show that the Huron clans were the older members of the group; and the clear and positive traditions of all the surviving tribes, Hurons, Iroquois, and Tuscaroras, point to the Lower St. Lawrence as the earliest known abode of their stock."

If the evidence presented in this paper be considered sufficient to justify the belief that the Cherokees entered the Ohio valley from the west, we are, then, forced to one of two conclusions, which may be stated briefly as follows: first, that this tribe, breaking away from the family in its eastern home, wandered westward, passing between Lake Superior and Lake Huron into what is now Wisconsin, and onward to the border of the plains, turning thence southward to the point on the banks of the Mississippi where we first find them; or, second (which is far more likely), the original stock was at one time in the distant past located in the region north-west of Lake Superior, and while here the Cherokees separated from their brethren, and moved southward to the banks of the Mississippi, while the latter, being pressed onward, moved eastward, north of the Lakes, to the banks of the St. Lawrence. If this supposition accords with what really was the direction of the movement, then it is highly probable, that, when they reached the Ottawa River, a portion followed down its course, while others turned southward into what is now Ontario, and were in that section when the Lenape appeared on the scene.

The first of these suppositions presents a movement so unlikely, though not entirely without a parallel in Indian history, that we feel constrained to reject it, so long as there is a theory consistent with the known data that is more simple and reasonable.

The evidence presented by Mr. Hale in the "Iroquois Book of Rites" leaves no doubt that the earliest known seat of the Huron-Iroquois family was on the Lower St. Lawrence; but it is scarcely presumable that their first appearance on the continent was in this eastern region. It is more likely that they had reached this point from some western section, and as they increased in numbers were forced to partially retrace their steps.

Although it is apparent that the authors of the ancient works east of the Rocky Mountains were substantially in the same culture state, and belong to the same race in the broad sense, yet there are some reasons for supposing (if we include the ancient works of New York under the general term "mounds") that the custom of building mounds originated independently in some two or three different sections. This is inferred from the fact that there appear to be at least three comprehensive classes of works: first, those of the Huron-Iroquois region; second, those of the Dakotan district; and, third, those of the southern section. These are not limited by ethnic lines, as the people who built the works along what we have designated the Cherokee and Shawnee belts probably derived the custom from the southern mound-builders.

The southern Dakotans, as the Quapaws and cognate tribes, also built mounds of the southern type. It is possible, however, that future discoveries in the north-west and south west may throw additional light on these questions, and modify the views here advanced, which are based, as a matter of course, only on the data so far obtained.

The attempt to estimate the time that has elapsed since the arrival of the Cherokees on the banks of the Mississippi (assuming the theory advanced to be correct) or since their meeting with the Lenape must be almost wholly conjectural. Mr. Hale says the time which has elapsed "since the Tallegwi were overthrown" is variously estimated, but that the most probable conjecture places it at a period about a thousand years before the present day, which would carry it back to the ninth century. Basing the estimate on the traditional evidence, for mound evidence gives but little aid in this respect before contact with the whites, it would seem to be more nearly correct to place the event in the eleventh or twelfth century. How long they had remained in this region when the war with the Lenape occurred is a question that must be left wholly to conjecture until other data than those we now possess are obtained; but it must have been a stay of some centuries, during which, as before said, they had lived in comparative peace. There are some reasons for believing that during this time another tribe had pushed its way up the Ohio River to the region about the mouth of the Miami. It is even probable that bands had crossed to the north side of the Ohio, and established themselves along the banks of the two Miamis. These I am inclined to believe, as heretofore remarked, were Shawnees who probably entered the Mississippi valley after the advent of the Cherokees. There is some evidence, however, in this region, of the presence of another small tribe which must have been driven out or destroyed. The remains which indicate the presence of this tribe are peculiar stone heaps and stone graves. It is possible that the presence of other people in this part of the Ohio valley caused the Cherokees to retreat up the Kanawha instead of southward across Kentucky.

CHAPTER VIII.

THE importance archæologically of the questions here discussed does not end with their bearing upon the history of a single tribe, for at almost every point there are side connections with other peoples. If it be admitted that the Cherokees were mound-builders down to the appearance of the white race on the continent, the mystery of the builders of our ancient monuments is virtually dispelled; for the lines which radiate from this point are so numerous and so far-reaching, that, when traced out to their utmost extent, the whole realm of mound-builders will have been traversed. This is a view of the subject which has not received due consideration on the part of those who admit that some of the works are attributable to Indians, yet claim that others are due to a different and more highly cultivated race. An illustration by partially tracing one or two of these lines will serve to impress the reader with the importance of investigation in this direction.

Reference has already been made to the fact that engraved shells similar to those found in the mounds of North Carolina and East Tennessee have been discovered in stone graves of a particular type, and that stone graves of this type often occur in mounds assigned, even by disbelievers of the Indian theory, to the true mound-building age. As the designs on these shells are peculiar, it is reasonable to conclude that the builders of the two classes of works were contemporaneous, or that there was an overlapping to some extent chronologically. Following up this line, which is traceable by other indications than merely the form of the sepulchres in which the dead were buried, we are led in one direction to the banks of the Delaware, where, history and archæology inform us, the Indians of that locality were burying their dead in tombs of the peculiar type mentioned, as late as the time of William Penn. It carries us in another direction, to southern Illinois, where links are found connecting unmistakably with the historic tribes of that section.

Going back to the Cumberland valley, the chief seat of these stone-grave builders, other lines start out which lead to the ancient works of south-eastern Missouri. Speaking of objects taken from "the peculiar stone graves of the Southern States," especially those of the Cumberland valley, Professor Putnam states that he has classed these "as belonging to the southern mound-builders, from the fact that the careful exploration of thousands of the graves, under the direction of the Museum, shows that their contents, including the human remains, are of the same character as those of the burial mounds in general, in the same region. . . . We have conclusive evidence, in the objects here arranged, that the stone-grave people of the south-west, and at least one group of the mound-builders, were one and the same people."

In another place he says, "Many of these carved disks of shell have been found in the graves and mounds of Tennessee and Missouri, and, with the identity of the associated pottery from the two localities, go far to prove the unity of the people, notwithstanding some slight differences in burial customs."

Although it is probable that Professor Putnam is not justified in concluding that the people of the two sections were tribally identical (if this be his meaning), yet the strong similarity in the forms, ornamentation, and character of the pottery leaves no doubt that they were contemporaneous, and, in consequence of contact or intercourse, had adopted in some respects similar customs.

Thus it is seen, that, commencing with the mounds of the Cherokee district, the connecting lines lead to the modern and non-mound-building tribes of the Delaware valley, to the historical tribes of Illinois, and to the veritable mound-builders of middle Tennessee and south-eastern Missouri. Nor do these complete the list of points to which the branches of this single diverging line lead us. As there are other diverging lines, it is apparent, that, when all have been traced out along their various branches, a large portion of the mound area will have been traversed.

This renders it highly probable that there was no manifest break in the mound-building age. It may have continued, and probably did, for many centuries, but there is no satisfactory evidence found in the monuments that there were two distinct mound-building ages. On the contrary, the historical, traditional, and archæologic testimony is decidedly in favor of the theory that our prehistoric works are attributable to the Indian tribes found inhabiting this country at its discovery, and their ancestors.

www.ingramcontent.com/pod-product-compliance
Lightning Source LLC
Chambersburg PA
CBHW020158170426
43199CB00010B/1094